RETAIL SHRINK 101

Books Coming Soon From this Author

Retail Management 101 The Truth
Retail Standards and Expectations
Pulling Out Employee Potential
10 Keys to Retail Success
Examining the Content of Character
Defining What is Right
Universal Success in Management
Strategies in Becoming a Manager

Publishing
Musically United Academy Inc.
P.O. Box 92593
Nashville TN, 37209
For more information go to:
www.retailshrink101.com
To request seminars or other training material and books concerning retail management contact: 1clearpurpose@gmail.com

RETAIL SHRINK 101
Theft Prevention

for the small box retail industry

Joel Santana
Editor—Troy Richardson

iUniverse LLC
Bloomington

RETAIL SHRINK 101
Theft Prevention

Copyright © 2013 by Joel Santana.

All rights reserved. No part of this book may be used or reproduced by any means, graphic, electronic, or mechanical, including photocopying, recording, taping or by any information storage retrieval system without the written permission of the publisher except in the case of brief quotations embodied in critical articles and reviews.

iUniverse books may be ordered through booksellers or by contacting:

iUniverse LLC
1663 Liberty Drive
Bloomington, IN 47403
www.iuniverse.com
1-800-Authors (1-800-288-4677)

Because of the dynamic nature of the Internet, any web addresses or links contained in this book may have changed since publication and may no longer be valid. The views expressed in this work are solely those of the author and do not necessarily reflect the views of the publisher, and the publisher hereby disclaims any responsibility for them.

Any people depicted in stock imagery provided by Thinkstock are models, and such images are being used for illustrative purposes only.
Certain stock imagery © Thinkstock.

ISBN: 978-1-4759-9854-2 (sc)
ISBN: 978-1-4759-9855-9 (ebk)

Printed in the United States of America

iUniverse rev. date: 08/02/2013

CONTENTS

Introduction ix

Shrink 1
    What is Shrink? 1
    How do we reduce shrink? 3
    How to train our employees 6

Difference Between Theft & Shrink 8
    Theft is wrong! So what do Retailers do about it? 8
    How do we identify petty theft and control it? 9

Getting Results 11
    How do Retailers create great shrink results? 11
    How do we attempt to reach Retailers forecast goals? 12
    How do we retain customers? 12

Industry Comparisons & Standards 14
    Upholding company policies 14
    Facts and Opinions . . . how does this relate to shrink? 15
    What are the shrink problems small box Retailers face? 17
    What are the issues high shrink stores face? 17

Preparing Your Staff 19
    How do managers create shrink preventing employees? 19
    What do managers need to know? 20
    Potential Customer Risk Behaviors 21
    Employee Potential Risk Behaviors 23
    Vendor Potential Risk Behaviors 24
    Strategies of Awareness 25
    How are great shrink results created? 26

Discussion 27
    There will always be something new to teach 27
    Laws that pertain to shrink 27
    Applying the Law 28

Keys Toward Controlling Shrink 30
    Keys to control Shrink... 30
    What are employers looking for on applications
        or in the interview process? 31
    Are employers wasting their time hiring this potential
        employee? 32
    Training employee's to prevent shrink 46

Appendix The Laws That Pertain To Shrink.................................. 49
    Bill of Rights.. 49
    Transcript of Civil Rights Act (1964) 50
    Tennessee's State Laws 80

Work Cited.. 89

This book is dedicated to God,
and the sacrifices of our Lord and Savior Jesus Christ.

The Enemy Comes to Kill, Steal, and Destroy
But Jesus came that we might have life and that more abundantly.

INTRODUCTION

This book taps into many elements of retail shrink exposing the darkest and deepest fears toward overcoming it. The author having over ten years of retail management experience gives readers and Retailers all the essential tools and keys toward obtaining successful shrink goals. This non sugarcoated work gives not only the truth but an objective and nonobjective view in resolving potential shrink issues. The content of this book is in no way intended to be misleading. This book is designed to teach its readers by guiding them into making sound decisions and freely exploring endless possibilities. In this book the author speaks vividly about his own personal failures and victories. Only through these real life experiences can a book like this be made to touch every facet of shrink. Not only does the author identify the problem but delivers concrete solutions. The content of this book contains; facts, suggestions, ideas and personal experiences. Readers be wise and use "what applies" to your situation.

SHRINK

What is Shrink?

Shrink is the difference between book inventory and physical inventory. Book Inventory is when a retail store purchases inventory for their store. The products purchased now belongs to them and becomes recorded in their book inventory. Physical Inventory is a retail store's purchased product that is now physically in their store for sale. The difference between what the store inventory books says and what the store can physically count is called shrink. Shrink is normally associated with a loss yet, by definition shrink can be classified as a growth or a loss in the retail market. What we want to be focused on is not only how shrink occurs but, how to prevent and reduce the wide gap of shrink from forming. Many shrink problems derive from these four main categorizes.

- Accounting Errors
- Accidents
- External theft
- Internal Theft

Accounting Errors| Let's examine the categories starting with Accounting Errors. Shrink that is caused by paperwork discrepancies can create small and large losses. A few small losses caused by paperwork discrepancies involve errors in the charges or credits made by vendors, distributors, customer returns, cashier errors, register data integrity, markups, markdowns, services rendered, and clerical errors. These small losses can add up quickly if not properly monitored and quickly corrected. Large losses caused by paperwork discrepancies can involve the same charges and credits mentioned above, but simply have high dollar amounts attached to them. These amounts entail the charges or credits of an entire truck load of merchandise that may or may not have been received. Products or services of this nature can happen if left unchecked. Most paper work errors can be fixed if caught early by simply creating good practices and procedures. This means retailers must create a system in place to verify and resolve these charges and credits on a regular basis.

Accidents | Accidents can create shrink losses. Normally there are three types of accidents that occur; an employee accident, customer accident, and/or sub-contractors being injured. Sub-contractors are employees of a separate company that provide a product or service to another company. Subcontractors can be injured while providing a service or a product. If an injury happens on-site the Retailer must investigate the validity of the claim and resolve the issue professionally. Employees that become hurt while on the job can also create shrink issues. An employee injury could occur at any time within the work place. It is hard to foresee what type of injury may occur. If good habits are not enforced an accident will possibly be the end result. Finally, customers who visit or shop at a retail store can be injured as well. These injuries can be caused from a variety of ways. Retailers must do all that they can to safe guard the potential risk of accidents. Sometimes resolving these accidents can be quite costly but normally Retailers purchase insurance to offset these costs.

External Shrink | External Shrink happens when Retailers allow people outside of the company to shop, visit, or conduct business in the store. During this time individuals who take financial or tangible assets illegally without prior approval create external shrink. This type of potential shrink can occur quite often and becomes very unpredictable. Statistics state 14.4% of theft is contributed to external theft while 70% is internal theft. Prevention techniques can be applied to this form of shrink and can be quite effective if used properly. If handled incorrectly lawsuits and negative publicity can start to form. Potential profit loss, business loss, and the loss of employees can also be the result of failing to act according to the law.

Internal Shrink | Internal Shrink is another form of loss. Internal Shrink is caused by dishonest employees and/or sub-contractors. During employment these individuals take it upon themselves to do what is wrong instead of what is right. They take financial and tangible assets without prior approval. Internal Shrink has been one of the highest contributors to shrink. The access and shear carelessness costs retailers millions of dollars over long periods of time. Retailer expectations should be in the best interest of the customer and the company. If they hire individuals to work they expect them to perform in a way that does not diminish the company's vision and goals. Retailers hire employees and subcontractors with the intent to grow or sustain their business. Unfortunately all employees and subcontractors are not honest and hardworking individuals. Though systems are in place to prevent or detour theft these systems can be broken down over time. Before we can examine how these systems are broken down we must understand the logical reasoning behind theft or the intent to steal.

People steal for numerous reasons. Some reasons may seem plausible and justified, but regardless of reasoning and justification—theft is WRONG and illegal. As a society we will be held accountable for our actions according to the law. Theft can be contributed to many different factors. Theft can stem from depression, financial instability, marriage issues, unforeseen losses, careless attitudes, opportunities that present themselves, and many more reasons. Though Retailers initially devise theft preventive systems to ensure good habits and practices are in place, Retailers understand theft cannot be eliminated nor can it be completely prevented. History and experience has made it known that no matter what is said or done theft is inevitable. The truth of the matter is if a person wants to steal they will no matter what. So, our true purpose is not to think we can eliminate theft but to try and reduce the amount of shrink that may or may not occur.

How do we reduce shrink?

This is the question we would all love to know. Some Retailers may think they already know the answer. But, do they really? There are a lot of retail store managers out there creating good shrink numbers within their district but unfortunately every retail store manager is not controlling their shrink. I have been in retail management over 10 years and I know the struggles store managers go through each day. If Retailers believe they are doing a good job. Then I say excellent way to go! Know what? This book is not for you. Please ask for a refund or something because this book is not meant to create good retail shrink numbers. This books' true intent is to turn shrink numbers into the best they have ever been or ever will be. So if this is not you. If somehow you do not believe you can do it or it can be done then stop! Because if you have been listening to what people have said you are and belief them and you extend your faith toward nonsense then stop! Because no one can help you because you are unwilling to help yourself. Think about it! OK, if you want to be the best then let's go because I am prepared to endow you with wisdom I wish I knew years ago. This is the new way of identifying potential shrink and having the knowledge of what to say and what to do to prevent shrink. This knowledge and wisdom is something that I wish I knew before I became a retail manager.

Please understand in order to control shrink. Retailers must understand the foundational principles in which they must endow in order to fight against it. Preventive methods may be in place to assist retail managers to reach their set shrink goals. But, the fact of the matter becomes weather or not retail managers are being empowered and are empowering others to do the same. What is happening in the small box and large box retail industry is the lack of knowledge which can create fear and doubt. Retail managers are not truly educated on all aspects of shrink. They may understand the definition of retail shrink and how it can devastate store profits. They may even think they have an excellent full proof system in place to prevent it. Unfortunately Retailers are lacking to teach a few necessary preventive methods and procedures in order to eliminate the unnecessary problems they incur.

It is fascinating to see Upper levels of management such as: District Managers and Regional Managers become uneasy when an experienced store manager becomes relocated. Upper levels of management have been convinced that in order to control shrink they must keep store managers in the same store to create a proven shrink record. I believe this to be FALSE. I agree sometimes it can be challenging for inexperienced store managers to pick up where a well experienced manager has left off. The condition of the store may suffer but controlling shrink should not be an issue. If new managers were trained and empowered to do what is right for the customers and the company. This shrink dilemma would not arise. There may be a lot of adjusting required in order for a new store manager to manage a new store. But does this mean that shrink prevention cannot be sustained through this transitional period? Does this mean that the store manager is the sole entity required to prevent shrink? These questions become puzzling to think that one person is the sole proprietor of shrink prevention. Understand that the reason why good retail shrink results can happen are not because of one person working and doing what is expected of them. It is simply the character and standard embedded within that one person willing to do the right thing no matter what—then affecting their environment and atmosphere to do the same. In order to make this change a person must be willing to compose their character and raise their standards. This composing becomes habit forming. I have over heard store managers state that they know if Upper levels of management put history proven shrink performing store managers in any store then that stores shrink problems would reach or exceed company shrink goals. This would mean that experienced managers would be able to control any retail store's shrink regardless of current or past shrink failures. Now there may be many elements concerning the validity of this claim and the truth thereof. However disputed it may seem I do believe if a store manager is happy in a store they will do well. But, they will only do the best they can to the best of their ability. So if Upper levels of management are under the impression that potentially they run a higher risk hiring a new store manager and an equal loss of relocating an experience store manager. What can be done to fix this? What can Upper levels of management do to fix shrink sustainability?

I remember working at a large box retail store. I was an entry level manager fresh and new to the management world. At this store we had Walkies-talkies as our form of communication. One day while working at this store. I overheard my manager stating that there was a problem at the front entrance door. I rushed to meet her to see what was going on. When approaching the scene I noticed our loss prevention sales associate and assistant manager arguing with a customer. I also noticed there was another man idly observing what was going on. The two customers were in fact together; the woman arguing and the man standing idly by. I didn't know what I was supposed to do. I was there to help but to what extent? I didn't know what was happening due to my lack of knowledge concerning potential shrink but this was an attempt to control shrink in progress. While observing the situation hostile words were simply escalating until my assistant manager and loss prevention associate decided to knock the customer down. During the scuffle the customer resisted and it took several minutes to control her on the ground. My co-workers frantically asked me to help them—frozen in shock I did nothing! After another minute I finally called the store manager to come resolve the situation. At this time the man standing idly by decided to go outside to a car which happened to be conveniently waiting right outside the door. Now there were three potential risks; the woman on the ground, the man standing idly by, and the person driving the "getaway car". The man standing idly by left before the store manager came to the scene by this time the customer was already pinned down on the ground. My assistant manager and the loss prevention associate were piled on top of the customer. The customer finally gave up. So my co-workers proceeded to pick the customer up off the ground since the store manager arrived to assist them. The assistant manager and loss prevention associate recovered all the merchandise and proceeded to detain the suspect. The management team cheered as they took the customer in hand held hand cuffs to the LP office. During that time and sometime after the incident my managers and co-workers exclaimed at me "Why didn't you do anything. Why didn't you help us hold her down? The man even got away. You should have made him stay, or at least you could have written down the license plate number." I felt as if somehow I let my team down. I failed to act accordingly but, I didn't know what to do nobody told me. Nobody trained me.

How to train our employees

What are we supposed to do in a theft situation? So many retailers have given their employees different ideas and suggestion on how to handle a customer theft or robbery situation. But are they truly giving employees all the necessary information and tools to become successful? I have been in at least 50 shrink meetings in my career. I have been taught the definition of shrink. Little things I can do to prevent shrink. Ideas on how to handle customer theft. What I am not supposed to do? Retail policy and procedures were all different at every company. They would teach me how to conduct myself while preventing shrink. The retail company would make sure to tell me what not to do so the company would not get sued. I have been told how they want me to handle a theft situation. They told me what I could be fired for. I was also told that if I do not find a way to control the shrink in my store I will be fired too. So, what does all this mean? It means when it all comes down to it, either I do something about shrink or get fired for not doing enough. Each retail store has its own shrink preventive system. Each Retailer uses shrink preventive methods to reduce or control shrink. Retailers even create policies to promote prevention. Please understand that I intend to break most or all retail policies and go for what really matters most the law.

The law supersedes all store policies and procedures. Laws are in place to level the playing field for all mankind. We have laws in place to make our society and way of life "fair" for all. The law does not want be to be taken avenge of and the law has no respect of person. The law is intended to give citizens of the United States equal rights. We have many laws in place but the most important laws are the constitution of independence, the 10 amendments to the constitution, civil rights, federal laws and state laws. When citizens of the United States get out of hand these laws bring society back into rightful order. These laws supersede store policies, procedures, and ethics. No matter what happens these laws are what you and I, as law abiding citizens of the United States will be judged and prosecuted by. So if this is true then why are Retailers not fully using these laws to empower their people to do the right thing?

DIFFERENCE BETWEEN THEFT & SHRINK

Theft is wrong! So what do Retailers do about it?

Retailers simply ignore the fact that customers are stealing? "If you didn't see it didn't happen." a loss prevention manager told me one time. Retailers refuse to take a stand and chose to do something about it? State law says that stealing is against the law so how can Retailers enforce this law? There are hundreds of ways. Let's talk about some of these ways. First let us talk about the different types of customer theft. Classifying the most important and relevant forms of theft in the retail industry would be:

- Attempted robbery
- Armed robbery
- Petty theft

Attempted robbery is when a customer or thief attempts to take the financial or tangible assets from a person or property without prior approval. This type of robbery is normally unsuccessful. It is merely attempted. The hope of theft is to steal without being caught and suffer no consequences resulting from the crime committed. But, during the scheme of things this type of robbery becomes unsuccessful. In the attempt to rob someone or something someone gets caught or evidence is captured due to poor planning. If victims or citizens acting in good judgment report these findings to the proper authorities the law can prevail. It is only if the proper steps are made that suspects are found and the financial or tangible assets are recovered. Only through this process can the law and justice prevail.

Armed robbery is bit different than attempted robbery. Usually a gun, knife, bat, or blunt object is used to give the robber support. This support gives the robber leverage to be more confident in thinking that the robbery will be more successful. This type of robbery tends to create a more hostile and aggressive atmosphere. The danger imposed can be devastating with an incalculable amount of damage resulting. Thinking about or having to go through this type of ordeal can be a very emotional roller coaster. Armed robberies do happen in the retail world and can be unexpected and unpredictable. Plans should be in place in order to handle any and all types of theft. This would entail store measures assisting in reducing large opportunities for theft to be evident and teaching employees what do before, during, and after a robbery.

In order to prevent theft Retailers must understand the root problem. The root problem is the internal and external components that are connected to theft. One major component of external theft conflicts and intertwines with the counter part of internal theft. This theft is called petty theft.

Petty theft is when someone takes small amounts of financial or tangible assets from a person or property without prior approval. Petty theft must be looked at from all different angles from slow to rapid shrink losses that become evident. What may seem like small amounts of losses starting off soon become major losses over an extended period of time.

How do we identify petty theft and control it?

Petty theft can be identified as being the result of customers, employees, vendors, visitors, contractors, subcontractors or anyone taking financial or tangible assets from a company. Once Retailers have identified and realize that anyone may or may not be a threat they must find a way to identify who they must watch. Preventing theft is not a once a week thing. It is not an every other day thing. Preventing theft should be a habit forming consist reaction of controlling shrink. If correct and well taught preventive practices are in place. Then, controlling shrink becomes a natural and non-subconscious reaction to controlling shrink.

As an example: If a retail store manager had a cashier and properly taught them how to operate the register the cashier would be able to continually operate the register to the best of their ability. During the times the cashier was operating their register. They may mess up or even forget in part how to operate the register. It would be the retail managers' responsibility to remind the cashier to perform their register operating responsibilities. The manager would have to start by showing the cashier the Intermittent cashier register operating procedures. After consistent practicing the cashier would form a habit of operating the register. It may be good habits it might be poor habits either way habits are formed. Then a natural or non-subconscious reaction of operating their register would occur.

If this example is true then all preventive procedures could be taught and made to be good solid habit forming techniques.

I can remember managing a retail store and naturally identifying potential threats to shrink and also shopping at other retail stores and identifying their potential threats to shrink. This habit was formed intentional and non-subconsciously due to the methods and teaching atmosphere I created within my own store. It took me a minute to realize what was happening because not only was it happening to me. But, my entire store was affect by this phenomenon. I would hear stories from my cashiers and co-workers that worked within my store. They would come to me and tell me the potential shrink risks they assessed by shopping at other retail stores. In fact they had such a conviction within themselves that they told the managers running the retail store what they were doing wrong. I am not sure what the management team did concerning the few shrink issues my co-workers identified. But, I am sure a customer telling a retail manager a problem concerning their store only becomes heard minutely to most managers. Either way at this point I knew something had happened to the fabric of our store and it was good, matter of fact is was great!

Every retail store and Retailer has a basic philosophy. This philosophy is simple. Retail is retail no matter where you go or what Retailer you work for. Retail is all the same. What concerns the retail industry the most is shrink and sales or sales and shrink. Retailers can put these words in any order they want. But, as a retail manager somehow if these to two concerns Retailers have are not met then, perhaps retail is not a smart career choice to be in pursuit. Unfortunately this book is not designed to teach managers how to obtain great sales. This book is designed to teach managers or potential manages how to create excellent shrink results which can help promote sales.

GETTING RESULTS

How do Retailers create great shrink results?

Retailers must create an atmosphere to prevent shrink. Retailers may think their current shrink prevention system is good. They may have even developed a solid preventive method to control shrink already. Retailers may believe there is nothing new to learn because their stores have been performing really good shrink numbers for years. Good for you Retailers. This is great, way to go I am glad to hear it. At this time I need everyone to pay close attention including managers and/or potential managers. At this point time is money and money is being wasted under those current systems. Either conform and understand the true revelation of what is happening in retail stores abroad or be naive and become the norm. Loss prevention managers have acknowledged many relevant problems to shrink. They have assessed that each retail store holds it's own set of obstacles and hurdles it must jump to gain, and maintain specific shrink numbers. Retailers also already know that shrink is going to happen and that it cannot be eliminated. This obvious conclusion has forced Retailers to create budgets that forecast potential shrink goals to accountant for losses.

Forecasting shrink budgets vary from store-to-store. Retailers must understand and acknowledge the demographic issues that arise in each store they open. Retailers naturally gravitate to specific locations within in a city to attract their market audience. Pending on the nature of their retail business the location can make or break the success of a business. Retailers try to focus their attention to their market audience. A market audience can be anyone from children, men, woman, or football fans, whoever they believe will benefit or desire to purchase the products they are selling. After research has been established for their potential market audience, and a suitable location is found. Retailers will decide either to open a store or not. If they do decide to open a retail store they must factor in all the potential problems or successes that may or may not occur within in that business. So Retailers create a forecast budget based off of studies and research. Now, it is up to all the levels of management to attempt to reach that goal or exceed that goal once Retailers have decided what those numbers should be.

How do we attempt to reach Retailers forecast goals?

This is when it can get a little tricky. Retailers are expecting managers to do everything they can to run the business well. They give managers the tools and training they feel can prepare them to succeed. Through the training process managers learn different retail company policies and procedures. Retailers even go the distance to teach relevant state and government laws. They do this to educate and inform managers of the extended expectation beyond their store parameters. These government laws supersede store policies and procedures. Managers are expected to obey these laws regardless of the situation or circumstances they may encounter. Store policies can be broken and are broken on a daily basis. Whether or not Retailers want to admit to their own inconsistency in store polices the statement is true. Retailers #1 goal is to take care of the customer. Retailers want to be fair and just when taking care of their customers. Retailers' true intent is to make customers happy on a consistent basis in order to retain their market audience. If they fail to do so they believe customers will stop shopping at their business and reevaluate their options. Retail competition is fierce. Retailers know if customers are unsatisfied with the products and excellent service they should provide they might lose that customer. The customer might leave and find another store for a brief time or they might leave permanently.

How do we retain customers?

Every customer is different. They have different needs, wants, desires, and personalities. Retailers have to be sensitive and willing to adapt to these four unique customer traits and needs. In order to accommodate customers Retailers must be able to adapt to customers wants, needs, desires, and personalities. It is hard to find a proven method to accommodate all of these traits. But, Retailers must attempt to do their best. In this endeavor Retailers teach their managers how to merchandise their store, maintain the stores appearance, and how to handle all customer problems and complaints. Retailers have policies and procedures they enforce in order to create equality. This uniform equality is to prevent inconsistency, favoritism, and to protect company assets. These policies and procedures are not always in the customer or Retailers best interest to follow. So instead of losing valued customers and potential sales, Retailers change policies and procedures. By doing this they eliminate the possible problems of losing their customer base and not proficiently protecting their company assets.

INDUSTRY COMPARISONS & STANDARDS

Upholding company policies

I do not encourage managers to intentionally break company policies and procedures. I encourage managers to voice their opinion to Upper levels of management to create changes in poorly designed policies and procedures. It is not hard to know when to break policies. The question managers must ask is not if they should break company policies but why they should break company polices. This is what separates the reasoning of right from wrong. In most states there is a law called Employment at Will. This law plainly states employees have the right to leave or terminate their own employment with or without cause. Also as employers-employers have the right to terminate their employees with or without cause. At this point nobody's job is secure or safe. If managers are already fearful in doing what is equally right for their customers and equally good for their business. Then, they are already slowly stuck in a negative downward spiral. If employers already have the power to terminate employment with or without cause managers which were hired to contribute and assistant in the overall vision of the business now become hindrances. If mangers are not helping the business then they are hindering the process of improving what may be a poorly woven thread stitched in political fabric. The fabric of policies and procedures. Most managers desire to be great managers. They want to help to improve the store and the company vision. Unfortunately sometimes they just do not know how because no one has taught them. If Retailers truly empowered their managers and told them they had the right to do whatever they wanted in order to manage their store. The atmosphere would immediately change. Retailers cannot be foolish stating that their managers will not be held accountable for their actions. This is not smart. This is not the essence of empowerment. The essence of empowerment is when Retailers tell their manager's yes we have polices, we have procedures, and also yes managers do not to forget about state laws, federal laws, civil rights, constitutional rights and any and all government laws and rights. At this point then Retailers could tell managers that all these laws, rights, and policies will still remain the same. But now managers as qualified leaders and contributors can choose what they believe is fair and right based off the law. Retailers could reassure managers by not terminating them immediately but assisting them by coaching to improve their beliefs. How much power would employees hold? How would managers feel about this new found freedom and system?

Facts and Opinions . . . how does this relate to shrink?

At this point say that Retailers decide to utilize this method of empowerment. Now the fear managers once had no longer exists. Managers are free to do whatever they want and are fully taught all the laws, rights, and policies that apply to their job. They are fully aware and understand there may or may not be ramification for their actions. Also through all their bad decisions they have the right through due process to explain the reason behind their decisions. After their decision is made due process will develop the outcome of being innocent until proven guilty and to help towards fixing errors in judgment. This is what lawyers call a fair trial. If this foundation is built Retailers can examine and teach methods on how to use this new found power and freedom. Regardless of what might seem to be a fact or an opinion let managers decide how to use these facts based off of laws and policies and to determine their own fate based on empowered actions. Retailers can terminate employee with or without cause so managers should know why and how they can or will be terminated before it happens.

Now that managers know the law and company policies how can this be used to prevent shrink? Shrink is a long list of do's and don'ts. Retailers can talk about shrink and find a million ways to identify the reason shrink exists. How Retailers choose to fix or reduce these shrink issues is up to them. Retailers who really want to see a difference in yearly shrink results must teach this secret to every manager and make sure their managers are teaching their co-workers the same. Empowerment: Every employee has to be empowered to prevent shrink. Retailers know this is true they just do not know how to convey the message.

Let me talk about another story before we dig deep into this subject. I personally have been to over 50 shrink meetings. I have listened over and over from store managers, district managers, loss prevention managers so on and so forth about shrink. I have been given the statistics of shrink. I have heard what managers are not allowed to do because of the law and how Retail companies have and can be sued.

I have heard the strategy of using the method—if management has not witnessed a theft and has lost visual contact with the customer. The manager is not allowed to approach the customer and question the customer concerning potentially stolen merchandise. If managers did so they may be fired if the customer did not steal the merchandise or have the merchandise in question. Managers were required to identify specifically what the item was and point out exactly where the merchandise is being concealed. I was told if I did not see it, it did not happen. Loss prevention managers have told me if I can see the merchandise hanging out of a customer's purse or body that I am allowed to take it by force. Suggestions that were made to help to prevent shrink were—"aggressive customer service". If I am aggressive in my customer service skills and make the customer aware of the fact that I know what they are doing. This exposure would detour or prevent a potential act of theft because thieves do not like to be noticed. In these meetings managers would go over invoices, refund frauds, a list of preventive measures from checking the alarms, changing safe pass-codes, watching video surveillance, using anti-theft stickers, gator tags, EAS tags, sensors, alarm sensors. Discrepancy on paperwork reports that could raise the flag of a potential shrink concern. Through all these meetings the biggest thing that I learned was simply theft is wrong and employees should be fired. Customers should be prosecuted if they choose to steal, and all managers should check and double check all preventive measures that were taught in order to prevent shrink. I even heard about how we should involve our employees and co-workers to be involved and knowledgeable about all of the retail practices and procedures in place to prevent shrink. How managers have to use these prevent measures to protect retail stores and make sure our team members are helping us to do the same. I am going to tell everyone the truth. I think these preventive measures may work OK for large box retail stores. But, this is truly not going to be as effective for the majority of small box retail stores. A lot small box retail stores penetrate the market in hopes to capitalize on the white collar and low income family demographic. Urban and high crime areas benefit a great deal from the local Dollar General, Family Dollar, and Dollar Tree type retail stores. The small box retail industry generates billions each year in sales and continues to grow. It is evident that the small box retail industry, market investors, and communities enjoy having small box Retailers in their communities. This becomes a win-win situation for everyone. But, statistics, research, and along with demographics retailers can tell they must to do more in order to prevent shrink in their retail stores. Retailers acknowledge that some locations within certain cities place their retail stores at a higher risk than other retail stores. In order to control the shrink of retail stores that is classified as high risk. Retailers must fight harder and fight smarter. There seems to be a larger set of controls in a high risk store than there are in low risk stores. These larger sets of controls are: live security, more cameras, more teaching, training, report monitoring, and many other conventional and unconventional theft prevention methods. Unfortunately Retailers do not know exactly how to go beyond the normal shrink preventive methods they have learned and retaught over so many years. Retailers continue to try to reinvent the shrink prevention wheel. But, this wheel seems to never roll in the right direction based on results and shrink failures there has not been a 100% successful full prove shrink prevention method until now. Retailers success can easily be measured by the financial state of not consistently reaching forecast shrink goals. So today everything is going to change. After the small box retail industry reads this book and applies the content thereof. They will finally know what is happening inside their retail stores. The retail industry will also be able to identify the true reasons behind poor shrink results and be able to identify, address, mentor, and reposition their shrink position in any and all stores. This book takes away the need to put certain store managers in certain stores to prevent shrink. This book levels the playing field for all retail managers to be successful in their endeavors to prevent shrink. Retailers listen and hear me loud and clear the shrink guessing game is over!

What are the shrink problems small box Retailers face?

First before unveiling the secrets that exist in order to prevent shrink. Let's address some of the big problems retail store managers face in their endeavors to prevent shrink. Retailers must hone in on major high shrink stores. They must attempt to fix the retail stores with high shrink issues before attempting to critic good shrink preventing stores.

What are the issues high shrink stores face?

High shrink retail stores face a careless customer and employee base. It is harder to retain a quality well equipped employee. When the threat of violence and carelessness is exuded from customers on a consistent basis, store managers are faced with huge hurdles and difficult obstacles to overcome within this type of environment. In this environment store managers must hire strong unafraid individuals who are willing to speak their mind and are not afraid of confrontation but can easily relate to others. Finally, employees must care about all aspects of the business including shrink. It is hard to mentor individuals that do not care about all aspects of their job. Careless employees are not afraid to tell their employer that they are just there for a paycheck. This is there true intention just to work enough to get a paycheck. Store managers must invest the time to find potential employees that want to do more, be more, and employees that are not afraid of finding ways to accomplish goals. If hiring is currently not an option then mentoring and holding employees accountable for their actions must become the store manager's number one priority. If employees are not willing to meet or exceed the expectations of the company then Retailers must let them go. In a situation of this magnitude employers do not have to do anything. Employees that do not care will simply leave on their own accord if standards and expectations are raised. Now since those employees who had perhaps low character, low standards, and no desire to use their true potential job position are now available. Now employers have an opportunity to hire shrink preventing potential employees. I would rather teach an employee from scratch-how to work or manage a retail store instead of trying to retrain a stubborn employee who has no desire to attempt to learn to give themselves a fighting chance.

PREPARING YOUR STAFF

How do managers create shrink preventing employees?

The same way employers can give their managers the power to do whatever they want. Managers within the retail environment must give their employees the right to do whatever they want. This is called empowerment. Retailers must enable everyone within their store to be empowered. Retailers are not losing control of their store by doing this. They are simply educating employees first then helping employees to truly be independent and to make good decisions. Think about this. When parents have kids they teach them life lessons as they grow older. Lessons of life could be conveyed in many different ways. One way could be the lesson of do not touch the stove when it is hot. Naturally children are curios and curiosity may gravitate them to make decisions they feel like making. So depending on the circumstances and environment created some children will chose to listen to their parents. Some children will take the initiative and touch the hot stove and become burned. The idea behind this is the fact that people will do whatever they want regardless of the outcome. Some will listen and obey good judgment. Others will not and will have to be burned once or many times before realizing the consequences of their actions. Maturity and character plays a large part of what people will or will not do. But if and only if people do not know the consequence of their actions can they really be held totally accountable for their mistakes. As an example if the children that were trying to play with the stove knew the consequences beforehand would the amount of children being burned be lessened than those that are not educated. Think about the educational system. Statistics and research has shown and proven that a college graduate will make more money in their life time than a high school graduate. Also, statistics have shown that obtaining a Master's Degree will significantly increase the probability of making more money through one's lifetime than a non-graduate. These are statistics and statistics always have a margin of error. The obvious ways to examine these facts are to know people that can testify to these truths. I personally know people who have a degree in a particular field of study and still do not make more than a high school graduates wage based on statistics. Bill gates the inventor of Microsoft dropped out of college and became the richest man in the world. Steve Jobs the inventor of apple computers dropped out of college and made more in his life time than most college graduates will ever. Knowledge is power it simply depends on the person and the support they are given that will determine how well their decision making ability will be. So Retailers must give their employees the right and the choice to make positive and negative decisions. Knowing what is in the best interest of the company and for the customer at times maybe difficult. I had a retail manager tell me two things that have stuck with me my whole life. He said this, "Do what you think is right and if for some reason it's not right then apologize for it later." He also asked me in my career if I knew what integrity meant. I attempted to answer his question and after I was done speaking he said "Integrity is doing the right thing when no is looking" and I believe as long as managers do these two things with the intentions of wanting what is best for the customer and what is best for the company everything will be fine. I tell my co-workers, "As long as you don't kill anything, you don't steal nothing, or destroy anything everything is going to be just fine." In order for empowerment to happen managers must first be educated. So what do employee's need to know.

What do managers need to know?

First, managers and employees need to know the laws. These documents have been taught in high schools, and colleges all across the world.

- The United States Constitution
- Federal laws
- State Laws (within the jurisdiction of the stores operations)
- Company Polices
- Any law or policy that could or could not directly affect employees as individuals as a whole, or the retail company period

These laws and policies must be readily available and understood in a context that is relevant to shrink situations that may occur. If these laws and policies can be applied then retail employees need to know the rights they have and the rights their customers have. Managers must be taught and mentored into having integrity and good character in order to lead properly and efficiently. My pastor told me, "Don't let your talent take you where your character can't keep you." If Retailers are unable to build and mentor the character of their managers and employees then maintaining great standards becomes very difficult. The first lesson of empowerment is having and building great character. If great character can be established then great decisions can be made and maintained. Managers can say and do whatever they want but if poor character is evident then poor shrink results and decisions become evident over time as well. Retailers must have managers that are willing to stand on what is right and not wavier no matter what. If the law is given then we must obey the law. If the law is broken then violators must be held accountable according to the law. Shrink must be realized to be by every employee as an unacceptable habit. Retailers must unveil shrink's one and only goal which is to steal, kill, and destroy the hope of retail success. Shrink cannot be tolerated in any form it presents itself. All employees must be empowered to address it accordingly. They have to start watching and listening to the ways and inclinations shrink can generally start forming. Let's specifically identify shrink from its possible intent.

Potential Customer Risk Behaviors

- ✓ Customers with bags or large purses
- ✓ Customers that consistently look at you while shopping
- ✓ Customers that set off the magnetic sensor detection device when coming into the store
- ✓ Customers that set off the magnetic sensor when leaving the store
- ✓ Customers that come in large groups then spread-out
- ✓ Customers that come in the store and walk around for long periods of time
- ✓ Customers that talk a lot while in the store
- ✓ Customers that seem to be nervous or afraid while shopping
- ✓ Customers with large purses and the zipper is unzipped
- ✓ Customers with money in their hand while carrying large purses
- ✓ Customers that act fake and try to be over friendly
- ✓ Customers that say "why you watching me I don't steal"
- ✓ Customers that say "I'm going to call cooperate because every time I come in here you're always watching me or following me around the store"
- ✓ Customers who become mad for no reason

- ✓ Customers that say "I don't steal—you want look in my purse?"
- ✓ Customers with baggy pants or overalls
- ✓ Customers with large coats when it is warm outside
- ✓ Customers that walk around the store counting money
- ✓ Customers that ask dumb question or need irrelevant information
- ✓ Customers that attempt to flirt or hit on you while their friend is shopping
- ✓ Customers that have flat purses when they come in and have bulky purses when they leave
- ✓ Customers that have a large purse and pretend to shop then walk to the register and say "I forgot my money or credit card in the car. I'll be right back" and then they don't come back
- ✓ Customers that enter the store wearing hats and glasses
- ✓ Customers that enter the store with hooded coats attempting to conceal their face.
- ✓ Customers that appear to be fake and too nice
- ✓ Customers that don't want to be bothered or noticed
- ✓ Customers that talk a lot for no reason and seem to be wasting employee's time
- ✓ Customers with rude or bad attitudes
- ✓ Customers that ask for change
- ✓ Customers that pay with large amounts of change or rolled coins
- ✓ Customers that seem to try and make a hostile work environment
- ✓ Customers that walk in the store and don't buy anything and leave in 5min or less
- ✓ Any customer that makes an employee uncomfortable or insecure while performing their job
- ✓ Customers that ask about people stealing in the store or ask about the policies and procedures
- ✓ Customers that always call and ask who is working today
- ✓ Customers' friends or family asking to know the schedule of an employee
- ✓ Customers that ask employees where employees are in the store
- ✓ Customers that try to return merchandise without a receipt
- ✓ Customers that always seems to be returning items of high dollar value

- ✓ Customers that carry a large purse and have their money in their hand
- ✓ Customers that wear layered clothing
- ✓ Customers that hang out in the health and beauty or the chemical aisle and only buy food
- ✓ Customers that start walking funny in the store
- ✓ Customers that do not want help or to be bothered
- ✓ Customers that want to use your bathroom a lot
- ✓ Customers with unregistered paper plates on their car.
- ✓ Customers that have someone waiting in the car outside for them.
- ✓ Customers that act like they know you

Employee Potential Risk Behaviors

- ✓ Employees with a poor attendance record
- ✓ Employees that do not want to be asked to do things
- ✓ Employees that say "that's not my job"
- ✓ Employees not willing to clean the bathrooms.
- ✓ Employees that seem timid or afraid
- ✓ Employees that always have an excuse
- ✓ Employees unwilling to do what the company expects from them
- ✓ Employees with poor cleaning habits
- ✓ Employees that always seem to be lying or not telling the full truth
- ✓ Employees unaware of their surroundings
- ✓ Employees that seem to talk a lot and are not genuine
- ✓ Employees that don't seem to care about anything
- ✓ Employees who take frequent smoke breaks
- ✓ Employees that have bad attitudes and are not friendly
- ✓ Employees that do not want to talk about their business
- ✓ Employees that always seem to be hiding something
- ✓ Employees that do not let employers check their bags when coming in the store or leaving the store
- ✓ Employees that have low self-esteem that have no goals they are pursuing
- ✓ Employees who talk about you behind your back
- ✓ Employees that say one thing and do another
- ✓ Employees that have no desire to better themselves
- ✓ Employees that have low patience and cannot trust anyone

- ✓ Employees that can't control themselves in a hostile situation
- ✓ Employees who always text, or are always on their cell phone or company phone
- ✓ Employees that eat or use merchandise without a receipt
- ✓ Employees that think it is OK to steal
- ✓ Employees who believe employers should not fire or prosecute people for theft
- ✓ Employees with no self-respect or respect for others.
- ✓ Employees that are dressed inappropriate and do not care about their appearance
- ✓ Employees that don't care about what people think because they're going to do whatever they want to do
- ✓ Employees that don't follow shrink preventive measures and policies
- ✓ Employees that don't ever catch people stealing
- ✓ Employees that never talk about theft or how to prevent it
- ✓ Employees that don't take any initiatives
- ✓ Employee that don't like to follow the rules
- ✓ Employees that only want to lead and never follow
- ✓ Employees that don't take creative criticism well
- ✓ Employees that find it hard to listen to authority
- ✓ Employees that are always stressed out about personal problems
- ✓ Employees that always seems to trust people

Vendor Potential Risk Behaviors

- ✓ Vendors that seem to be in a rush
- ✓ Vendors that seem to talk a lot or be distracted
- ✓ Vendors that seem overly friendly
- ✓ Vendors that tell retail managers while processing deliveries that they will evenly exchange their credits with new merchandise without creating another invoice receipt
- ✓ Vendors that ask weird uncommon questions
- ✓ Vendors that seem lazy and unproductive
- ✓ Vendors that only want to do the mere minimum
- ✓ Vendors that feel like they don't have to listen to anyone and they can do whatever they want
- ✓ Vendors that like to take short cuts.
- ✓ Vendors who seem nervous or uncomfortable when auditing the legitimating of their merchandise counts

- ✓ Vendors that always want to use your bathroom
- ✓ Vendors that always seem to hang around when their job is done
- ✓ Vendors that bring unnecessary bags or boxes in the store
- ✓ Vendors who don't seem to care about their job or others
- ✓ Vendors that always have a bad attitude
- ✓ Vendors that don't like anybody.
- ✓ Vendors that feel people can't be trusted

The list could go on and on. Now that retail employees can identify potential shrink risks. They can now teach other employees or co-workers how to "ring the alarm". Managers must find a system to raise the alarms concerning potential risks. It is a waste of time to know what could be a potential risk if no one is going to do anything about it.

Strategies of Awareness

All retail employees have to be aware of what is going on in their store. Each and every employee must participate in Shrink Awareness. They not only have to be aware of potential shrink risks but they must also have the authority and knowledge to know what actions to take. Knowledge is power and power has the ability to make fear go away. Just imagine if a car dealership representative asked a regular person on the street to build them a car. The dealership representative does not plan it out. They just go downtown and pick a person at random. The person they pick is just an average Joe. So the representative walks up to the potential prospect and says, "Hey how would you like to work for me." Surprised the person says, "Me? Why me? The representative says, "Why not?" The potential prospect says, "I'm just an average Joe." The representative says, "Great Joe the car dealership that I work for wants you to build them a car." Average Joe tells the car dealership representative, "I don't know how to build a car." The representative says, "that's OK Joe were going to teach you everything you need know we'll even pay you. Heck will even tack on some incentives and give you a hefty salary." At this point average Joe becomes all ears. Average Joe says "What if I mess up and somehow it doesn't work out, plus it'll probably take a long time to learn to build a car." The representative reassures Joe and says, "It'll be fine you won't mess up. We'll help you get it done as long as you try your best and do exactly what we teach you. The car will end up looking great and be exactly what we imagined it always could be." Average Joe considers the proposition and the fact that this could be a joke and says, "Why not? Let's see what happens. Deal me in. I'll build the car." Alright so how are we going help average Joe? This is what we are going to do. Instead of having average Joe build a car were going to have average Joe build Retailers great shrink results.

How are great shrink results created?

Great shrink results are created by teaching employees everything they need to know about shrink. Employees must know what shrinks is. How shrink is created. Where shrink comes from and how to control and reduce shrink losses? Retail employees need to know the forecast shrink goals of the store they work in. They need to know the shrink history of their store. They need to know that they cannot trust anyone in the store and that they cannot be trusted. This does not mean people are not trustworthy. It simply means people must prove it daily through actions not words. They need to know how to identify potential risks. Last but not least they need to know that they are supported and empowered to fight against shrink with or without the companies help. Once all this is explained and is out of the way employees and managers together can fight against shrink.

DISCUSSION

There will always be something new to teach

Teaching the basic shrink methods and preventive procedures are very important. But they are not as important as knowing the extent of every judicial law and policy that can pertain to shrink. If Retailers simple taught each and every employee the United States law, State laws, Federal laws, company policies and any other law pertaining to shrink. Employees would be better prepared in order to fight against it. Retail employees do not want to feel as if their job will be in jeopardy in their effort to prevent shrink. Retail employees at all times want to know their efforts are making a difference and they want to know what those differences are. They want to know how shrink preventing methods are measured. They want the retail company they work for to update them on the progress of those measurements. If Retailers are willing to empower their employees and teach them how to make great decisions shrink prevention will succeed. Retail employees cannot be made to feel like they are going to be hurt in the process of preventing shrink. They need to plainly understand what they will or will not be fired for. They need to know and feel confident that they are not being forced to put themselves in danger. This danger reflects the actions of being physically hurt, emotionally hurt, or reprimanded for intentionally trying to help the company within the extent of the law.

Laws that pertain to shrink

Think about these laws the right to privacy, search and seizure, loitering, soliciting, the freedom of speech and how they relate to shrink prevention. Before explaining how to utilize them they all must be taught and learned. These are just a few that I mentioned. Just imagine if every retail employee had an opportunity to study them all. Actually not an opportunity but had to know their legal right before attempting to abolish shrink.

These laws are intended for law abiding citizens of the United States of America. These laws are intend to make what could be devastating wrong decisions and actions into equal rights for all so that citizens of the United States do not become victims and are taken advantage of. So citizen and Retailers of the United States let us use the power which has been bestowed upon us to make sure no one takes these rights away from us. So citizens of the United States of America let us do what is fair and right for all mankind. Retailers and retail employees declare and decree making a proclamation that nothing and no one will continue to take advantage of Retailers and retail employees. The shrink goal set forth by our retail companies will and shall become achievable and obtainable each and every year. All shrink issues will be overcame by all forms of shrink preventive methods no matter how important or insignificant. This day is the day that shrink gaps begin to close.

Applying the Law

The last and final step toward impacting and preventing shrink is how to put it all together and have it make sense. The preventive methods should now be in place. Our retail managers and employees should be well educated in shrink, in the law, and company policies. Everyone is at liberty to do what is right for the customer and what is right for the company. It is time to prevent shrink and apply the law. Retailers must lay down some basic and general rules to follow before identifying a potential shrink issue. Checklists that are helpful in the process of reducing shrink must be enforced and continued. Checklists would consist of regular and routine audits on;

- Cash management procedures
- Video surveillance protocol
- Theft preventive tagging and sensory
- Accident prevention methods
- OSHA standards and regulations
- Being ADA complaint
- Food safety regulations
- Food freshness programs in place
- All inventory control methods
- All store delivery preventions and verification methods
- Fraudulent financial customer transactions awareness forms
- Key handling controls and accountability

Retailers can continue to add to this list and take away from this list as they so choose. After this list is assessed, complied, and taught Retailers can move forward and teach the major and most important shrink preventive method. These methods makes the difference between winning and losing. It makes the difference between being a good shrink controlling retail store to a excellent shrink controlling retail store. These methods can take an uncontrollable shrink performing store into a shrink controlled atmosphere. Finally, down to the "nitty-gritty" creating the shrink preventive wall within the store and the wall that surrounds the outside of the store.

KEYS TOWARD CONTROLLING SHRINK

Keys to control Shrink

First key towards successfully controlling shrink is hiring the right people for the job. It is very easy to know if Retailers have hired the right people to work at their stores. These employees would be considered solid employees. Retailers have to hire employees that want to do more with their lives. Solid employees are individuals that want to move up in the company or want to learn all they can in order to reach their own personal success. If Retailers hire individuals that just want to work to receive a paycheck then ding-ding Retailers have identified the wrong potential employee. Retailers must be willing to train potential employees without worrying about if that employee will leave within six months to a year. Employers never really know what a potential employees' true intentions are when hiring or interviewing them. Employers try to ask all the right questions such as;

1. Why does the potential employee want to work at the retail company they have applied for?
2. Work availability
3. Wages desired
4. Work history
5. Educational background
6. Goals the potential employee endeavors to accomplish
7. Criminal background
8. If the potential employee can pass a Drug test
9. Employers should verbally create real life customer scenarios to judge whether or not a potential employee can or has made good work related decisions
10. These scenarios can involve
    a) Employee theft
    b) Customer Theft
    c) Time management
    d) Problem solving skills so on and so forth

By this time the interview is over the employer should have a strong idea if the potential employee is worth considering or can at least be capable of performing the job expectation they have applied for. This end result is called mutual compatibility. The employee can express verbally what they are capable of doing concerning productivity. What they have experienced in the past through previous employers and how they handled those experiences. The potential employee also can talk about what they plan on doing in the future. All these techniques and questions are very important to the employer. Based off the interview an employer can assess their risk of hiring a potential employee.

What are employers looking for on applications or in the interview process?

To make this short, employers look for work experience, availability, educational background, work history to determine the experience and willingness of a potential employee to stay with the company for a long period of time. This willingness to stay employed should be about a year or longer. Criminal Background information and drug test results give employers ideas to the extent of poor decision making that an interviewee may have made. Potential applicants may make poor decisions after hired if this aspect of the application is not properly investigated into. But the most important part of the interview process, and this is not to take away for the relevance to the initial questions but to enhance the big overall picture is this question. What do you plan on doing in the next 3-5 years? This is the most crucial part of the entire interview process. All the rest of the questions are very important but out of all the questions this question is the most important. In order to prevent shrink this question must be asked and thoroughly discussed. Where do you see yourself in 3-5 years? I am sure employers would argue to say the criminal background, drug test; customer and employee theft questions are more important and related more to shrink prevention than future goals. I beg to differ and this is the reason why. I agree that a potential employees past can affect their ability to perform their job and possibly represent a form of bad judgment. It can also affect their work habits and ethical position on certain subjects. But if a potential employee wants to change and better themselves they can and will. Now if I ask a potential employee as far as employment is concerned, what they plan on doing in 3 to 5 years from now and they tell me they want to be an astronaut. I might ask them what they are doing in order to reach that goal. If they tell me nothing then it is obvious to me they do not know how to reach their goal, or they are not serious, nor do they intend to attempt to better themselves in that aspect of reaching their personal goals. So at this time I am not sure if the potential applicant is worth the time to be considered for a job. Now if I ask that same question to an applicant. I ask them what they see themselves doing in the next 3 to 5 years. If they say I want to be in health care administration. At this point I assess how compatible retail management is to health care administration. If I wanted to dig deep into the cross references that relate health administration to retail management, I would assess; time management skills, delegation skills, paper work proficiency, the ability to multitask, and the stress of maturity and responsibility. I would consciously assess the compatibility healthcare administration has based off the job responsibilities in retail. So, say I find a match. This person now has realistic goals. Possibly say that the interviewee tells me that they are going to school for healthcare administration or believes a job in retail management can help them pursue their personal goal toward being a healthcare administrator. If the applicant has a short or spotty work history and I assess based off of work history the longevity of this potential employee is the value of six months of consistent employment. I would have to ask myself is it worth the time to invest in a potential employee that possibly will only be with the company for six months? This could be a tough question for any retail employer. If a employer interviews an applicant that meets all the basic requirements in the interview process and the applicant is willing to work the hours needed, passes the background check, drug screening, then the employer should ask the applicants about their future goals. Employers should think to themselves and challenge themselves toward helping others purse their personal goals. A lot of good results can be generated from hiring a potential employee that wants to do something with their life. Employers should want to help potential employee's pursue their own personal goals. Especially if the goal is toward the same or similar skill set given or learned in the field of retail.

Are employers wasting their time hiring this potential employee?

Most Retailers would say "Yes" not hiring this person would be better because employers would just be wasting their time. It would be in the company's best interest to find someone that wants to be with the company for a long period of time." See Retailers want to hire potential employees that are willing to stay with their company and to them this can only be determined by someone who has a good long term work history. Employers do not want to hire an individual that just bounces from one job to the other. This statement is a valid point yet on the other hand some Retailers would say "No" because they believe that possibly the potential employee may change their mind and decide to stay with the company for a long period of time if given a chance. At the same token how can potential employees create a work history if no one is willing to give them a chance? At this point which employer is right and which employer is wrong. I'll tell you the answer but, first let me tell you a story.

As a young man still in college I had a lot of hopes and dreams. There were so many things I wanted to do with my life. I worked at a few different companies through high school; two months here three months there nothing consistent. Finally I got married and had to get a full time job. So at this time I had one years worth of college done in electronic technology. I went job hunting that year and applied to many different electronic stores and electronic technology companies. After a few interviews and very little luck I decided to apply for a job at a large box retail store. This large box Retailer offered me a job as an electronic sales associate. I thought to myself this is great. This job is in my field of study. I can help the company and the company could help me learn more about electronics. I worked there for about a year. I never intended to stay but after a while I got stuck working there for various reasons. Since I was stuck there I wanted to at least make more money. So when my year was up and it was time for my raise, I was excited to see what this Retailer was prepared to offer me after one years worth of work. I sat down with the assistant manager and the department manager of electronics. They talked about my performance, attendance, and how I could improve. They offered me a 20 cent raise. I was furious, 20 cents I replied! I worked all year for you to pay me $7.00 more a week. They asked me to calm down so they could explain some things I was doing incorrectly. They said I could help customers more instead of standing by the register. I could stock faster, recover the store better and come to work on time more and stop being late. I thought to myself I never missed a day of work. I thought yes, I may have been late a time or two but, so what! No one has wrote me up, coached me, or said anything about my performance. I did not understand how they were just going to criticize me all at once. They did not tell me anything prior to this meeting. I was unhappy, very unhappy, and I did not want to sign for my raise or my 1 year evaluation. I declared to talk to the store manager. The assistant manager told me, "fine I will arrange that." and that "I really needed to search my heart to what is fair and what is right." A few days past and finally they gave me my chance to sit down with the store manager. I was prepared to prove my case. We talked about my concerns, how I felt, and what was going on. Then the store manager pulled out some reports and began to speak about my attendance records and company policies. He stated "based off these reports I am surprised you're still working here." I felt dumb and had no proof but by my word concerning my attendance and it helped nothing. So from that day forward I decided to change. The weeks after this petty raise I started to work hard every day. I made sure I was never late. I made sure I worked every minute I was schedule. Upper management was so impressed they acknowledged my efforts and decided to move me up in management. I slowly began to move up in management. I received better pay. But, I was still not satisfied. I wanted to be an assistant manager or a store manager. I heard assistant managers made no less than $40,000 annually and store managers did not make less than $65,000 annually in this large box retail store. They even received hefty bonuses each year based on sales and shrink, I wanted that! I initially had no intention of being with the company for a long time but I thought I could do it and the pay sounded nice. When I interviewed for management positions that were intended to promote my career goals I was passed up for lack of experience. They felt someone else was more qualified than me. I did not understand or know what to do. I wanted to just quit and give up. But something inside of me wanted to be more. I knew I could do it. I knew I had the potential. I just needed a chance. I needed someone to believe in me. After a while I started venting toward my assistant manager asking for help and guidance to achieve their position. I had one assistant manager tell me this "if you want to be an assistant manager act like one, dress like one." The managers at the store would wear slacks a dress shirt and a tie. So after that day I wore slacks, a dress shirt and a tie. When I went to work my co-workers laughed at me. My store manager looked at me funny. My fellow co-workers made me feel like I was wasting my time and that I would never amount to anything. It took weeks possibly a few months before the management took me serious. Finally they gave me a management job that was intended to prep me into becoming an assistant manager. I worked really hard in my new management position. My job was inventory control leader. I was in charge of the backroom. I managed 15 employees and assisted them in making sure the trucks were unloaded properly. I gave out time limits in order to process freight, worked freight, and kept the stock room clean neat and organized. The backroom was my baby. I personally designed a plan in place for everything to get done. I made sure the back room standards were impeccable. If anyone failed to meet my expectations and standards, I personally made sure they knew it. If an assistant manager was responsible for messing up my back room I would call the store manager, if the store manager messed up the backroom. I would call his boss. My mentality was that no one was going to mess up my back room period. It did not take long before I had everyone's attention. I made sure not to do anything that would get me fired or at least give anyone a good enough reason to fire me. I can remember one day working as an Inventory control leader when the District manager came to visit. The District manager was their to evaluate the store standards. When he came into my stockroom I immediately addressed him and told him who I was. At this time the Store manager and Co-manager were walking with the District manager. I noticed that while they were walking in my stock room they did no want to be bothered. I attempted to walk with them. The management team gave me funny looks. They looked at me as if I did not belong. They did not want me to walk with them because whatever they were talking about was none of my business. Oh well, I did not care about their funny little looks. I told myself if they want to walk in my stockroom I was going to walk with them. If they wanted to talk about my stockroom then I was going to talk with them. When the District manager asked questions I would immediately talk to answer the question. I would not even give my Store manager time to respond. He did not know my backroom better than me. It was my baby I was the one taking care of it. So I was the one that was going to defend it. So the District manager asked "what are we going to do about this empty space here." I would say that space is designated for power panels or side kick displays. He would ask "how long has this merchandise been back here". I would tell him dates, times, and the plan that was in place to stock it to the sales floor. After walking my stockroom the District manager was so impressed he asked me to walk with him to the other side of the store. On the other side of the store the stock room was terrible. The management team tried to justify why but the District manager did not want to listen. He told them, "you need to send your inventory control leader over here to fix this side of the store so it looks as good as it looks in the other stockroom." I just smiled and tried to stop smiling but I could not help it. Before the tour was over the District manager asked if I knew about sales and shrink. He asked me to look at some reports in his hand. I did not know what he was talking about but I sure tried to act like I did. The District manager stopped the tour and made the Store manager and

Co-manager wait for him to explain report figures to their inventory control leader. These reports were something I did not know anything about. I still remember that day. After that happened my District manager made me an Assistant manager. I worked for that large box retail store for seven years before resigning. I would probably still be working there if it was not due to poor management. I eventually transferred to a store in a different city. I thought I was a great Assistant manager. At least this was what my Store manager and fellow Co-workers said I was. When I transferred to another store the entire atmosphere changed. All the employee's at this new store hated working for this new Store manager. I was not sure why until I worked there myself. This Store manager had about a 700% turnover rate per month The last five Assistant managers quit and the ones that were currently there wished they could quit everyday they worked. They felt like they did not have a choice they had to provide for their family. The problem was this Store manager wanted a perfect store and he did care what he had to do in order to make it that way. He would threaten employees that failed to do what he told them to do. He would fire them on the spot. All he talked about was how if someone was not performing in a capacity as well he could perform the job. He wanted to create an exit plan for them. It only took one day for him to assess an employee's termination. He thought in his mind the outcome of new employees and would openly say they were not going to make it. He wanted only the best or people that were better than him. I had never experienced this type of management in my life. Upper levels of management raved about his store standards and appearance yet they failed to see the efforts in place in order to obtain those standards. Needless to say I left that employer to move on to better myself, better my family, and to be in a better atmosphere. I could not accept only one form of management. Managing employees by treating them inferior like worthless cattle employed for one purpose "results." A management style forced labor such as this is ridiculous and short minded. It only took one person to believe in me for me to make it. I would rather invest all my time mentoring someone to succeed than spending a life time forcing people to create results. It only takes one person to make a difference. If it was not for people teaching and mentoring me to succeed I would have never been a manager. I would have never achieved the success I have had in retail if someone did not give me a chance. Success is developed through failures not instant successful results. Managers that are unwilling to be patience and properly mentor good, solid, and willing employees should not be managers at all.

So back to the interview process. If a potential employee believes they can be a manager or something more I believe Retailers should give them a chance. Employers really never know how long an employee will stay with their company. But, I am willing to bet that if an employer gave a potential employee a chance to be what they said they could be. Then that potential employee would work as hard as they could to prove it. Some potential employees that attempt this will fail. Some will fail and get up and will try and try again until they make it. The potential employees that are willing to try over and over again to better themselves toward their personal goals are shrink preventing employee's. Those are the employee's I want working for me in my store. I believe in pulling out every part of potential in every one I come in contact with. I have learned the more you are willing to help others with their personal goals the more they are willing to help you with your personal goals. So if I interview a potential employee and they say they have goals outside the parameters of being in retail. I tell them great! Those are the people I want to work with and be around. The employee's that only want to come to work to get a paycheck or just need a job are potential shrink risks. Poor character, poor integrity, poor performance, and the unwillingness to go above and beyond will be the end result. When I conduct an interview I want them to have goals. I want to know how I or my employer can help them achieve their personal goals. Retail companies have goals too. How does it sound for employers to force employees to help them achieve their goals and not have employers help their employees achieve their personal goals? If one goal is sacrificed to achieve a different goal then unsatisfactory performance will result sooner or later. No one likes to feel they have no purpose or they are stuck and never will fulfill their most inner hopes and dreams. So hire right by doing right for the interest of both parties. After employers have employees that have reasons to be there beyond company expectations, they can focus on more important things instead of solely worrying about shrink. This does not mean those potential shrink preventing employees won't steal from the company. It simply means it lessen the risk. This reduced risk is now helping to prevent shrink.

The second key to shrink prevention is simple. Let everyone in the store know that they cannot be trusted. If I am the employer do not trust me. If you are the employee I cannot trust you. Retailers and employees are here to work, not become friends. Knowing the definition of what is right and what is wrong can be clouded by a sense of trust within a working environment. Everyone is human and humans make mistakes. No one knows when that mistake will be made but they cannot trust that it will not be made sooner or later. Do not be naive

The third key is to know all the Government laws, Federal laws, State laws, Citizen Civil Rights and Store policies. Each one of these laws has to be taught and understood. Employers and employees really need to grasp there rights and know the authority they have. Retailers do not want people to take advantage of their retail stores. So Retailers, retail managers, and employees have to know what they can do to fight against those careless individuals that try and attempt to take advantage of retail stores.

The forth key is to be able to point out and identify potential shrink risk. The book has already talked about recognizing potential shrink risks it gives excellent examples to identify them.

The fifth key is that each retail store must have a secret pass word they use to identify potential shrink risks. This can be any word the employee's feel comfortable using. An example would be the word "hot" If there are two people in the store and an employee sees a potential shrink risk. They are to immediately notify everyone in the store concerning this potential risk. At this time they simple say, "it is hot in this store" to their fellow co-workers. At this time the alert is made and everyone should know there is a potential risk in the store. When handling a potential risk "NEVER" say to the customer or to an employee that a potential shrink risk is stealing or is a thief. It does not matter if it is a customer, employee, vendor, or a person simply visiting the store. "NO ONE" can be addressed as a thief until they have past the front door threshold which is classified as the point of no return. If the potential risk is still in the store they are NOT A THEIF! They simply may be concealing merchandise with the intent to purchase so employees must address the situation as what it is. Now if the potential risk has left the store without purchasing items then they are actually holding stolen merchandise whether it's accidentally or intentionally. Either way, "NEVER" address any individual as a thief or accuse them of stealing. Think of it as a judicial court the plaintiff is innocent until proven guilty. Let the law and courts examine the validity of this claim. Retailers cannot assume or make accusation that could possible end up being false.

Patricia A. Patrick and Shaun L. Gabbidon wrote a paper concerning false arrests. They state,

> "of the 235 cases studied, 63 percent were brought by shoppers who had been arrested for shoplifting, but had not actually shoplifted. In other words, more than half of the shoppers were arrested for shoplifting but were not caught in the act or found with stolen merchandise. Instead, they were arrested based only on the suspicion of shoplifting."

These false arrests can be devastating if individuals are accused of stealing or assumed to be a thief. Based on this statistic 6 of 10 people accused of stealing could be proven guilty according to the law. Patricia A. Patrick and Shaun L. Gabbidon go on to write and explain actual cases that happen concerning false arrest. They talk about what happened and what the outcomes were. These are two cases that actual happened.

> "In one case, an Arkansas woman was seen leaving a national discount-merchandiser with a 59-cent pen partially concealed in her pocketbook. She was acquitted at trial when she claimed that she had forgotten to pay for the pen. The jury awarded her $21,000 in damages because the security officers had failed to follow the retailer's established procedures for the detention, interrogation, and prosecution of at trial, the store manager said he was not familiar with these procedures and that he always prosecuted suspected shoplifters and left the issue of guilt up to the court. The court found that the store manager had grounds to stop the woman for questioning but that he should have used her explanation to help decide whether he should bring charges against her for shoplifting. He did not do that. Instead, he proceeded on automatic pilot without regard for company rules."

Based off of the United States 10 amendments of the constitution of independence it clearly states,

Amendment 1

Congress shall make no law respecting an establishment of religion, or prohibiting the free exercise thereof; or abridging the freedom of speech, or of the press; or the right of the people peaceably to assemble, and to petition the government for a redress of grievances."

Retailers at this point have the constitutional right to say whatever they want. For an example if a customer goes into a retail store with a large purse and decides to pick up some detergent and put it in their purse. The retail employee on duty has the right to ask the customer to take out the merchandise that belongs to the company. Employees should not accuse the customer of stealing. Employee's just simply have to ask the customer to take the concealed merchandise out of their purse.

Amendment 4

The right of the people to be secure in their persons, houses, papers, and effects, against unreasonable searches and seizures, shall not be violated, and no warrants shall issue, but upon probable cause, supported by oath or affirmation, and particularly describing the place to be searched, and the persons or things to be seized.

The Fourth Amendment to the Constitution clearly states people to be secure in their homes, papers, and effects. This would mean customers are not allowed to take or search a retail store's, documents, financial or physical merchandise without prior approval. Retailers are not allowed to take or search customers documents, financial or physical merchandise without prior approval. Retail managers can ask potential customers not to conceal merchandise in the store and to ask them to have their merchandise visible at all times. If employee's of a Retailer believe a customer is concealing merchandise they cannot physically take a customer's property such as; a purse, coat, shirt, or hat without prior approval. Retailers have the right not to sell merchandise to whoever they choose. Customers have the right not to let retail employees search or seize their personal possessions. In the event that a retail employee catches a customer concealing merchandise the employee has the right to ask for the merchandise back. If the customer refuses to cooperate or chooses to utilize their right not to open their purse or show proof of concealing merchandise whether it is on their body or personal property. Retail employees must obey the law and respect that. At this point if the customer refuses to cooperate with the retail employee, the employee should ask the customer to leave the store. The retail employee should make all the employees in the store aware of what is going on in the store while it is happening. The retail employee should tell all employees in the store to remember that customers face before the customer leaves because they are not allowed in the store anymore. The retail employee should call the police or have their co-workers call the police. The retail employee must make sure the customer leaves the company property completely. During this time the retail employee should gather all the information they can to give to the proper authorities. This would include the customer's physical description height, weight, sex, hair color, eye color, clothing the customer may have been wearing, including shoes. Any identifying marks such as tattoos or scars. The color, make and model of the vehicle. The license plate number and the direction the customer was going. All this information can be very helpful to the authorities. It would even help if Retailers created relationships with local Retailers to tell them when an occurrence has taken place. Please understand at no point is the customer considered a thief. They simply forgot or refused to pay for merchandise they concealed. Some Retailers would argue they cannot just kick people out of their store like that. They have to have proof. OK, well let's generate some proof or at least a solid justified reason beyond just making individuals leave. If Retailers review their state laws they would find a few laws concerning the rights for private property, loitering, soliciting, harassment, and controlling a hostile work environment.

Example 1:

If a customer continuously walks around the store employees have the right to ask the customers to purchase something or leave. This is called the law of loitering. If the customer refuses to buy something or refuses to leave retail employees can call the police to re-enforce this law.

Example 2:

Customers who come in the store trying to sell products or services are called solicitors. Solicitors can be asked to leave the store because of the law of solicitation.

Example 3:

Customer who act inappropriately in the store, such as cursing, making threats, throwing merchandise, looking at employees inappropriately, speaking with sexual innuendos, talking loudly, reorganizing store merchandise, running in the store, damaging products, customers tearing stickers off merchandise, and changing prices on merchandise.

All these are valid reasons to ask individuals that create a potential risk to leave. Retailers do not need to waste time trying to catch a thief. If this is what Retailers' intentions are "to catch thieves." Then that might be the reason why Retailers' shrink results are high or are only good enough. Retailers must understand they are supposed to prevent shrink in order to properly fight against it. Instead of waiting for individuals to create potential shrink let them give Retailers other reasons to kick them out. Retailers do not have to catch thieves to kick them out. They do not even need to address them as thieves to fix their shrink. If Retailers used all the techniques in this book Retailers would not even need to prosecute thieves unless, shrink derived from a internal problem and created a large loss in financial or tangible assets. Let's go back to the customer concealing merchandise. If the customer refuses to open their purse and refuses to leave the store unless they are allowed to purchase merchandise that is not concealed. The retail employee must reassure the customer that they will have to leave at that time. The customers unconcealed merchandise will not be rang up period. The retail employees must not allow customers that create a potential risk in the store to feel comfortable or give them any rights or privileges. Now that retail employee's know some of their rights and how to handle potential risks. How do employees prevent them from coming back?

There are few different ways. One way is filling out a no trespassing form concerning the potential risk in question. Also retail managers can empower and support their employees and use face recognition. If the retail store has a camera system that system may be able to create a picture album or some form of a loss prevention log to identify potential risks that are no longer welcome in the store. If any employee recognizes a reoccurring potential risk they are to tell that potential risk to leave the store immediately. If the potential shrink refuses to leave the store. Stating they do not know what they did. Then the employee is to state, "It has been brought to their attention that they are not allowed in the store." If the potential risk still refuses to leave and asks to speak with a manager on duty. The manager is to intervene and ask what is going on. If the retail employee that identified the potential risk states the potential risk is not allowed in the store then the manager supports their team member and reaffirms the request that the potential risk to leave the store. If the potential risk wants to know the reason behind the request to leave the manager on duty simply states, "They will have to investigate the validity of the claim and a member of management will get back with them as early as they can." If the potential risk still refuses to leave then the retail employee must call the police. Let the police do their job to force the potential risk to leave. If during this process the customer starts cussing or creating a hostile work environment employees can now use the cussing or inappropriate behavior as the reason behind the potential risk no longer "now" being allowed in the store. Retail employees have to make sure that they are all on the same page. The manager on duty cannot come in and intervene in the face recognition process and ask their fellow co-workers why the potential risk is no longer allowed in the store. This creates confusion and a lack of support. If this happens employees will not want help prevent shrink. Employees will no want to make a potential risk leave because they will not feel properly supported. Retailers and retail employees must support their co-workers decision and investigate later. This support is how retail employees maintain an environment of preventing shrink. Individuals that create potential shrink are very smart and very crafty. Many people have heard the slogan, "if someone wants to catch a thief first they must first think like one." If retail employees can identify potential risks and make them leave for good reasons. The only thing left to do is to give exceptional customer service. Retail employees must know who is in their store at all times. They must know what those people are doing in the store and why they are there. Individuals that create potential risks are very good actors. They want retail employees to think that they do not pose a threat. Potential risks will be kind, smile, and be well dressed. Do not be fooled by race, color, sex, religious beliefs, clothing, car, money or appearances. Retail employees have to be sensitive and look beyond all this and tap into the content of peoples' character. How is this done?

When an individual seems to pose a potential risk all employees are to be notified. One employee must approach the suspect and get to know them beyond casual conversation. Their use to be a television program on TV called the Pick-up Artist. Men or woman would find ways to talk to people through pickup lines. These men and women would have mentors teaching them through the whole pickup process. They would help the trainee become professional pickup artists. They would teach them how to start up a conversation. They would use words or subjects like "did you see that fight outside" or "do you like pickle juice?" to grab the attention of specific individuals they targeted as potential prospects. These conversation starters would help the trainee overcome the fear of not knowing what to say when approaching a potential prospect, after a while these pickup lines would become habit forming. The pickup artist would start the conversation, maintain the conversation, lead the conversation in the direction they wanted, and eventually get the potential prospects number or achieve something the pickup artist was attempting to get. Such as a kiss, time alone, or a date. So how can we use this information to start up conversations with individuals that create potential risk? How do retail employees maintain a conversation to find out a potential risks motives, intention, and goals? Then how do retail employees make the potential risk leave professionally without having any reason at all to kick them out of the store? Alright, so let's pick up our potential risks and find a way to kick them out with a reason or with no reason at all. Retailers want to achieve this result without creating any legality or poor customer service problems. If retail employees do not know what to say to individuals that possibly could create a potential risk. Ask potential risks these questions in the nicest mannerism.

Sample Ice Breakers

How are you doing today?	Can I get you a shopping basket?
Can I help you find anything?	Didn't you come in earlier?
Do you live far from here?	What is your name?
That is a beautiful purse.	Did you watch the news today?
I love your shoes where did you get them?	I don't know why people keep messing up my store
Nice shirt what does it say?	Aren't you Stacey's friend?
Where did you get that hat and glasses?	I called the police they're on the way are you OK?

Are you two sisters or cousins?	I think your car is being towed.
Do you shop here all the time?	I think someone hit your car outside.
Do you go to college around here?	I think your ride is waiting on you.
How old are you?	What high school did you go to?
Is that your car outside?	What is your name again?
Are you shopping all by yourself?	Do you know how to dance?
Do you like our new camera system it can see everything?	I have been catching people hide merchandise all day.
Did you drop something?	Why are you walking funny?
How long have you been shopping in the store?	Are you pregnant when is your baby due?
Let me show you our new products.	Is that your phone in your pocketbook?
Girl, who does your hair?	Why are your pants so bulky?
Do you think it's OK to steal?	Have you ever stolen before?

Training employee's to prevent shrink

These are just a few conversation starters retail employees can use. After a while the fear of talking leaves and the intimacy of knowing the content of someone's character can easily be revealed. Peoples inner most desire is not to lie. Most of the information given from the individuals that might create potential risk will be the truth. The truth maybe good it may be bad just never stop talking to the potential risk until they buy something or leave. If for some reason time and job responsibilities do not allow for casual conversation simply ask the potential risk if they need help. Take them to the item, count the item out loud so they know how many items are on the shelf. Let the customer shop and go and check to see if the item is missing, if evidence of empty packages are seen then DO NOT BE SCARED to use the 1 Amendment the right ask the potential risk what is going on. If the customer has unconcealed merchandise sticking out of their pocket take the merchandise and kick the potential risk out. If the potential risk says they picked up the item and then put it down. Make the potential risk proof it by taking the retail employee to the item in question if the item is not found. Then ask the customer to leave for misplacing an item or losing an item they said they picked up. Retailers must be very mindful of their rights and the rights of other U.S. citizens. Shrink prevention is on ongoing task and can only be best learned through trial and error. The best way of learning what not to do is by evaluating others attempting to tackle the same issues and not repeating their mistakes for example, Patrica A. Patrick and Shaun L. Gabbidon state,

> "In one case, an Indiana woman entered a large department store to return three sweaters that she had previously purchased. She carried the sweaters in a department store bag, but she did not bring the receipts along because the sweaters still contained the store tags, and she knew the store would allow an exchange without the receipts. However, instead of returning the sweaters immediately, the woman browsed through the store. She was eventually apprehended by two undercover private security officers and led to the store security office. During the apprehension, the woman dropped a blouse that she was intending to buy. One of the security officers picked up the blouse and placed it in her shopping bag along with the three sweaters. In the security office, the officers emptied the woman's shopping bag and her purse"

This a violation of the 4th Amendment of the constitution of Independence The customer was arrested on shoplifting charges it goes on to state,

> "The woman was acquitted of the charges and subsequently sued the retailer for false imprisonment, malicious prosecution, and defamation."

The jury awarded the shopper more than $1.3 million in actual and punitive damages. The retailer appealed the $1 million punitive damage award on the grounds that it was excessive, but lost the appeal."

Retailers must teach employees how to die-sect potential risk scenarios by role playing what could or could not happen within a fictitious scenario. Then they must apply all legality measures that could occur in every different scenario. Then give solid concrete solutions and answers for every possible outcome. This step takes a while and continues to be updated regularly based off of trial and error. Retailers must empower their employees and hire individuals with goals, good character, and standards. If any of these three elements fail to exist Retailers must invest the time and effort to fully develop their employees. This is the only solution in this consistently evolving retail industry. Shrink cannot be eliminated but it definitely can be controlled. Fight the good fight of faith and never give up. Excellent shrink results are obtainable.

APPENDIX
THE LAWS THAT PERTAIN TO SHRINK

Bill of Rights

The Bill of Rights
Amendments I-X (Adopted 1791)

Amendment 1
Congress shall make no law respecting an establishment of religion, or
Prohibiting the free exercise thereof; or abridging the freedom of speech, or of
The press; or the right of the people peaceably to assemble, and to petition the
Government for a redress of grievances.

Amendment 2
A well-regulated militia, being necessary to the security of a free state, the
right of the people to keep and bear arms, shall not be infringed.

Amendment 3
No soldier shall, in time of peace be quartered in any house, without the
consent of the owner, nor in time of war, but in a manner to be prescribed by
law.
Amendment 4
The right of the people to be secure in their persons, houses, papers, and
effects, against unreasonable searches and seizures, shall not be violated, and
no warrants shall issue, but upon probable cause, supported by oath or
affirmation, and particularly describing the place to be searched, and the
persons or things to be seized.

Amendment 5
No person shall be held to answer for a capital, or otherwise infamous crime,
unless on a presentment or indictment of a grand jury, except in cases arising
in the land or naval forces, or in the militia, when in actual service in time
of war or public danger; nor shall any person be subject for the same offense to
be twice put in jeopardy of life or limb; nor shall be compelled in any criminal
case to be a witness against himself, nor be deprived of life, liberty, or
property, without due process of law; nor shall private property be taken for
public use, without just compensation.

Amendment 6
In all criminal prosecutions, the accused shall enjoy the right to a speedy and
public trial, by an impartial jury of the state and district wherein the crime
shall have been committed, which district shall have been previously ascertained
by law, and to be informed of the nature and cause of the accusation; to be
confronted with the witnesses against him; to have compulsory process for

obtaining witnesses in his favor, and to have the assistance of counsel for his defense.

Amendment 7
In suits at common law, where the value in controversy shall exceed twenty dollars, the right of trial by jury shall be preserved, and no fact tried by a jury, shall be otherwise reexamined in any court of the United States, than according to the rules of the common law.

Amendment 8
Excessive bail shall not be required, nor excessive fines imposed, nor cruel and unusual punishments inflicted.

Amendment 9
The enumeration in the Constitution, of certain rights, shall not be construed to deny or disparage others retained by the people.

Amendment 10
The powers not delegated to the United States by the Constitution, nor prohibited by it to the states, are reserved to the states respectively, or to the people.

Transcript of Civil Rights Act (1964)
www.ourdocuments.govApril 18, 2013

Transcript of Civil Rights Act (1964)
An Act
To enforce the constitutional right to vote, to confer jurisdiction upon the district courts of the United States to provide injunctive relief against discrimination in public accommodations, to authorize the Attorney General to institute suits to protect constitutional rights in public facilities and public education, to extend the Commission on Civil Rights, to prevent discrimination in federally assisted programs, to establish a Commission on Equal Employment Opportunity, and for other purposes. Be it enacted by the Senate and House of Representatives of the United States of America in Congress assembled, That this Act may be cited as the "Civil Rights Act of 1964".

TITLE I—VOTING RIGHTS
SEC. 101. Section 2004 of the Revised Statutes (42 U.S.C. 1971), as amended by section 131 of the Civil Rights Act of 1957 (71 Stat. 637), and as further amended by section 601 of the Civil Rights Act of 1960 (74 Stat. 90), is further amended as follows:
(a) Insert "1" after "(a)" in subsection (a) and add at the end of subsection (a) the following new paragraphs:
"(2) No person acting under color of law shall—
"(A) in determining whether any individual is qualified under State law or laws to vote in any Federal election, apply any standard, practice, or procedure different from the standards, practices, or procedures applied under such law or laws to other individuals within the same county, parish, or similar political subdivision who have been found by State officials to be qualified to vote;

"(B) deny the right of any individual to vote in any Federal election because of an error or omission on any record or paper relating to any application, registration, or other act requisite to voting, if such error or omission is not material in determining whether such individual is qualified under State law to vote in such election; or
"(C) employ any literacy test as a qualification for voting in any Federal election unless (i) such test is administered to each individual and is conducted wholly in writing, and (ii) a certified copy of the test and of the answers given by the individual is furnished to him within twenty-five days of the submission of his request made within the period of time during which records and papers are required to be retained and preserved pursuant to title III of the Civil Rights Act of 1960 (42 U.S.C. 1974-74e; 74 Stat. 88): Provided, however, That the Attorney General may enter into agreements with appropriate State or local authorities that preparation, conduct, and maintenance of such tests in accordance with the provisions of applicable State or local law, including such special provisions as are necessary in the preparation, conduct, and maintenance of such tests for persons who are blind or otherwise physically handicapped, meet the purposes of this sub paragraph and constitute compliance therewith.
"(3) For purposes of this subsection—
"(A) the term 'vote' shall have the same meaning as in subsection (e) of this section;
"(B) the phrase 'literacy test' includes any test of the ability to read, write, understand, or interpret any matter."
(b) Insert immediately following the period at the end of the first sentence of subsection (c) the following new sentence: "If in any such proceeding literacy is a relevant fact there shall be a rebuttable presumption that any person who has not been adjudged an incompetent and who has completed the sixth grade in a public school in, or a private school accredited by, any State or territory, the District of Columbia, or the Commonwealth of Puerto Rico where instruction is carried on predominantly in the English language, possesses sufficient literacy, comprehension, and intelligence to vote in any Federal election."
(c) Add the following subsection "(f)" and designate the present subsection "(f)" as subsection "(g)": "(f) When used in subsection (a) or (c) of this section, the words 'Federal election' shall mean any general, special, or primary election held solely or in part for the purpose of electing or selecting any candidate for the office of President, Vice President, presidential elector, Member of the Senate, or Member of the House of Representatives."
(d) Add the following subsection "(h)":
"(h) In any proceeding instituted by the United States in any district court of the United States under this section in which the Attorney General requests a finding of a pattern or practice of discrimination pursuant to subsection (e) of this section the Attorney General, at the time he files the complaint, or any defendant in the proceeding, within twenty days after service upon him of the complaint, may file with the clerk of such court a request that a court of three judges be convened to hear and determine the entire case. A copy of the request for a three-judge court shall be immediately furnished by such clerk to the chief judge of the circuit (or in his absence, the presiding circuit judge

of the circuit) in which the case is pending. Upon receipt of the copy of such request it shall be the duty of the chief justice of the circuit or the presiding circuit judge, as the case may be, to designate immediately three judges in such circuit, of whom at least one shall be a circuit judge and another of whom shall be a district judge of the court in which the proceeding was instituted, to hear and determine such case, and it shall be the duty of the judges so designated to assign the case for hearing at the earliest practicable date, to participate in the hearing and determination thereof, and to cause the case to be in every way expedited.

An appeal from the final judgment of such court will lie to the Supreme Court.

"In any proceeding brought under subsection (c) of this section to enforce subsection (b) of this section, or in the event neither the Attorney General nor any defendant files a request for a three-judge court in any proceeding authorized by this subsection, it shall be the duty of the chief judge of the district (or in his absence, the acting chief judge) in which the case is pending immediately to designate a judge in such district to hear and determine the case. In the event that no judge in the district is available to hear and determine the case, the chief judge of the district, or the acting chief judge, as the case may be, shall certify this fact to the chief judge of the circuit (or, in his absence, the acting chief judge) who shall then designate a district or circuit judge of the circuit to hear and determine the case.

"It shall be the duty of the judge designated pursuant to this section to assign the case for hearing at the earliest practicable date and to cause the case to be in every way expedited."

TITLE II—INJUNCTIVE RELIEF AGAINST DISCRIMINATION IN PLACES OF PUBLIC

ACCOMMODATION

SEC. 201. (a) All persons shall be entitled to the full and equal enjoyment of the goods, services, facilities, and privileges, advantages, and accommodations of any place of public accommodation, as defined in this section, without discrimination or segregation on the ground of race, color, religion, or national origin.

(b) Each of the following establishments which serves the public is a place of public accommodation within the meaning of this title if its operations affect commerce, or if discrimination or segregation by it is supported by State action:

(1) any inn, hotel, motel, or other establishment which provides lodging to transient guests, other than an establishment located within a building which contains not more than five rooms for rent or hire and which is actually occupied by the proprietor of such establishment as his residence;

(2) any restaurant, cafeteria, lunchroom, lunch counter, soda fountain, or other facility principally engaged in selling food for consumption on the premises, including, but not limited to, any such facility located on the premises of any retail establishment; or any gasoline station;

(3) any motion picture house, theater, concert hall, sports arena, stadium or other place of exhibition or entertainment; and

(4) any establishment (A)(i) which is physically located within the premises of any establishment otherwise covered by this subsection, or (ii) within the premises of which is physically located any such covered establishment, and (B) which holds itself out as serving patrons of such covered establishment.
(c) The operations of an establishment affect commerce within the meaning of this title if (1) it is one of the establishments described in paragraph (1) of subsection (b); (2) in the case of an establishment described in paragraph (2) of subsection (b), it serves or offers to serve interstate travelers or a substantial portion of the food which it serves, or gasoline or other products which it sells, has moved in commerce; (3) in the case of an establishment described in paragraph (3) of subsection (b), it customarily presents films, performances, athletic teams, exhibitions, or other sources of entertainment which move in commerce; and (4) in the case of an establishment described in paragraph (4) of subsection (b), it is physically located within the premises of, or there is physically located within its premises, an establishment the operations of which affect commerce within the meaning of this subsection. For purposes of this section, "commerce" means travel, trade, traffic, commerce, transportation, or communication among the several States, or between the District of Columbia and any State, or between any foreign country or any territory or possession and any State or the District of Columbia, or between points in the same State but through any other State or the District of Columbia or a foreign country.
(d) Discrimination or segregation by an establishment is supported by State action within the meaning of this title if such discrimination or segregation (1) is carried on under color of any law, statute, ordinance, or regulation; or (2) is carried on under color of any custom or usage required or enforced by officials of the State or political subdivision thereof; or (3) is required by action of the State or political subdivision thereof.
(e) The provisions of this title shall not apply to a private club or other establishment not in fact open to the public, except to the extent that the facilities of such establishment are made available to the customers or patrons of an establishment within the scope of subsection (b).
SEC. 202. All persons shall be entitled to be free, at any establishment or place, from discrimination or segregation of any kind on the ground of race, color, religion, or national origin, if such discrimination or segregation is or purports to be required by any law, statute, ordinance, regulation, rule, or order of a State or any agency or political subdivision thereof.
SEC. 203. No person shall (a) withhold, deny, or attempt to withhold or deny, or deprive or attempt to deprive, any person of any right or privilege secured by section 201 or 202, or (b) intimidate, threaten, or coerce, or attempt to intimidate, threaten, or coerce any person with the purpose of interfering with any right or privilege secured by section 201 or 202, or (c) punish or attempt to punish any person for exercising or attempting to exercise any right or privilege secured by section 201 or 202.
SEC. 204. (a) Whenever any person has engaged or there are reasonable grounds to believe that any person is about to engage in any act or

practice prohibited by section 203, a civil action for preventive relief, including an application for a permanent or temporary injunction, restraining order, or other order, may be instituted by the person aggrieved and, upon timely application, the court may, in its discretion, permit the Attorney General to intervene in such civil action if he certifies that the case is of general public importance. Upon application by the complainant and in such circumstances as the court may deem just, the court may appoint an attorney for such complainant and may authorize the commencement of the civil action without the payment of fees, costs, or security.

(b) In any action commenced pursuant to this title, the court, in its discretion, may allow the prevailing party, other than the United States, a reasonable attorney's fee as part of the costs, and the United States shall be liable for costs the same as a private person.

(c) In the case of an alleged act or practice prohibited by this title which occurs in a State, or political subdivision of a State, which has a State or local law prohibiting such act or practice and establishing or authorizing a State or local authority to grant or seek relief from such practice or to institute criminal proceedings with respect thereto upon receiving notice thereof, no civil action may be brought under subsection (a) before the expiration of thirty days after written notice of such alleged act or practice has been given to the appropriate State or local authority by registered mail or in person, provided that the court may stay proceedings in such civil action pending the termination of State or local enforcement proceedings.

(d) In the case of an alleged act or practice prohibited by this title which occurs in a State, or political subdivision of a State, which has no State or local law prohibiting such act or practice, a civil action may be brought under subsection (a): Provided, That the court may refer the matter to the Community Relations Service established by title X of this Act for as long as the court believes there is a reasonable possibility of obtaining voluntary compliance, but for not more than sixty days: Provided further, that upon expiration of such sixty-day period, the court may extend such period for an additional period, not to exceed a cumulative total of one hundred and twenty days, if it believes there then exists a reasonable possibility of securing voluntary compliance.

SEC. 205. The Service is authorized to make a full investigation of any complaint referred to it by the court under section 204(d) and may hold such hearings with respect thereto as may be necessary. The Service shall conduct any hearings with respect to any such complaint in executive session, and shall not release any testimony given therein except by agreement of all parties involved in the complaint with the permission of the court, and the Service shall endeavor to bring about a voluntary settlement between the parties.

SEC. 206. (a) Whenever the Attorney General has reasonable cause to believe that any person or group of persons is engaged in a pattern or practice of resistance to the full enjoyment of any of the rights secured by this title, and that the pattern or practice is of such a nature and is intended to deny the full exercise of the rights herein described, the Attorney General may bring a civil action in the appropriate district court of the United States by filing with it a complaint (1) signed by him (or in his absence the Acting Attorney General), (2) setting forth facts pertaining to such pattern or practice, and (3) requesting such preventive relief, including an application for a permanent or temporary injunction, restraining order or other order against the person or persons responsible for such pattern or practice, as he deems necessary to insure the full enjoyment of the rights herein described.

(b) In any such proceeding the Attorney General may file with the clerk of such court a request that a court of three judges be convened to hear and determine the case. Such request by the Attorney General shall be accompanied by a certificate that, in his opinion, the case is of general public importance. A copy of the certificate and request for a three-judge court shall be immediately furnished by such clerk to the chief judge of the circuit (or in his absence, the presiding circuit judge of the circuit) in which the case is pending. Upon receipt of the copy of such request it shall be the duty of the chief judge of the circuit or the presiding circuit judge, as the case may be, to designate immediately three judges in such circuit, of whom at least one shall be a circuit judge and another of whom shall be a district judge of the court in which the proceeding was instituted, to hear and determine such case, and it shall be the duty of the judges so designated to assign the case for hearing at the earliest practicable date, to participate in the hearing and determination thereof, and to cause the case to be in every way expedited. An appeal from the final judgment of such court will lie to the Supreme Court.

In the event the Attorney General fails to file such a request in any such proceeding, it shall be the duty of the chief judge of the district (or in his absence, the acting chief judge) in which the case is pending immediately to designate a judge in such district to hear and determine the case. In the event that no judge in the district is available to hear and determine the case, the chief judge of the district, or the acting chief judge, as the case may be, shall certify this fact to the chief judge of the circuit (or in his absence, the acting chief judge) who shall then designate a district or circuit judge of the circuit to hear and determine the case.

It shall be the duty of the judge designated pursuant to this section to assign the case for hearing at the earliest practicable date and to cause the case to be in every way expedited.

SEC. 207. (a) The district courts of the United States shall have jurisdiction of proceedings instituted pursuant to this title and shall exercise the same without regard to whether the aggrieved party shall have exhausted any administrative or other remedies that may be provided by law.

(b) The remedies provided in this title shall be the exclusive means of enforcing the rights based on this title, but nothing in this title shall preclude any individual or any State or local agency from asserting any right based on any other Federal or State law not inconsistent with this title, including any statute or ordinance requiring nondiscrimination in public establishments or accommodations, or from pursuing any remedy, civil or criminal, which may be available for the vindication or enforcement of such right.

TITLE III—DESEGREGATION OF PUBLIC FACILITIES

SEC. 301. (a) Whenever the Attorney General receives a complaint in writing signed by an individual to the effect that he is being deprived of or threatened with the loss of his right to the equal protection of the laws, on account of his race, color, religion, or national origin, by being denied equal utilization of any public facility which is owned, operated, or managed by or on behalf of any State or subdivision thereof, other than a public school or public college as defined in section 401 of title IV hereof, and the Attorney General believes the complaint is meritorious and certifies that the signer or signers of such complaint are unable, in his judgment, to initiate and maintain appropriate legal proceedings for relief and that the institution of an action will materially further the orderly progress of desegregation in public facilities, the Attorney General is authorized to institute for or in the name of the United States a civil action in any appropriate district court of the United States against such parties and for such relief as may be appropriate, and such court shall have and shall exercise jurisdiction of proceedings instituted pursuant to this section. The Attorney General may implead as defendants such additional parties as are or become necessary to the grant of effective relief hereunder.

(b) The Attorney General may deem a person or persons unable to initiate and maintain appropriate legal proceedings within the meaning of subsection

(a) of this section when such person or persons are unable, either directly or through other interested persons or organizations, to bear the expense of the litigation or to obtain effective legal representation; or whenever he is satisfied that the institution of such litigation would jeopardize the personal safety, employment, or economic standing of such person or persons, their families, or their property.

SEC. 302. In any action or proceeding under this title the United States shall be liable for costs, including a reasonable attorney's fee, the same as a private person.

SEC. 303. Nothing in this title shall affect adversely the right of any person to sue for or obtain relief in any court against discrimination in any facility covered by this title.

SEC. 304. A complaint as used in this title is a writing or document within the meaning of section 1001, title 18, United States Code.

TITLE IV—DESEGREGATION OF PUBLIC EDUCATION
DEFINITIONS

SEC. 401. As used in this title—

(a) "Commissioner" means the Commissioner of Education.

(b) "Desegregation" means the assignment of students to public schools and within such schools without regard to their race, color, religion, or national origin, but "desegregation" shall not mean the assignment of students to public schools in order to overcome racial imbalance.

(c) "Public school" means any elementary or secondary educational institution, and "public college" means any institution of higher education or any technical or vocational school above the secondary school level, provided that such public school or public college is operated by a State, subdivision of a State, or governmental agency within a State, or operated wholly or predominantly from or through the use of governmental

funds or property, or funds or property derived from a governmental source.
(d) "School board" means any agency or agencies which administer a system of one or more public schools and any other agency which is responsible for the assignment of students to or within such system.

SURVEY AND REPORT OF EDUCATIONAL OPPORTUNITIES
SEC. 402. The Commissioner shall conduct a survey and make a report to the President and the Congress, within two years of the enactment of this title, concerning the lack of availability of equal educational opportunities for individuals by reason of race, color, religion, or national origin in public educational institutions at all levels in the United States, its territories and possessions, and the District of Columbia.

TECHNICAL ASSISTANCE
SEC. 403. The Commissioner is authorized, upon the application of any school board, State, municipality, school district, or other governmental unit legally responsible for operating a public school or schools, to render technical assistance to such applicant in the preparation, adoption, and implementation of plans for the desegregation of public schools. Such technical assistance may, among other activities, include making available to such agencies information regarding effective methods of coping with special educational problems occasioned by desegregation, and making available to such agencies personnel of the Office of Education or other persons specially equipped to advise and assist them in coping with such problems.

TRAINING INSTITUTES
SEC. 404. The Commissioner is authorized to arrange, through grants or contracts, with institutions of higher education for the operation of short-term or regular session institutes for special training designed to improve the ability of teachers, supervisors, counselors, and other elementary or secondary school personnel to deal effectively with special educational problems occasioned by desegregation. Individuals who attend such an institute on a full-time basis may be paid stipends for the period of their attendance at such institute in amounts specified by the Commissioner in regulations, including allowances for travel to attend such institute.

GRANTS
SEC. 405. (a) The Commissioner is authorized, upon application of a school board, to make grants to such board to pay, in whole or in part, the cost of—
(1) giving to teachers and other school personnel inservice training in dealing with problems incident to desegregation, and
(2) employing specialists to advise in problems incident to desegregation.
(b) In determining whether to make a grant, and in fixing the amount thereof and the terms and conditions on which it will be made, the Commissioner shall take into consideration the amount available for grants under this section and the other applications which are pending before him; the financial condition of the applicant and the other resources

available to it; the nature, extent, and gravity of its problems incident to desegregation; and such other factors as he finds relevant.

PAYMENTS
SEC. 406. Payments pursuant to a grant or contract under this title may be made (after necessary adjustments on account of previously made overpayments or underpayments) in advance or by way of reimbursement, and in such installments, as the Commissioner may determine.

SUITS BY THE ATTORNEY GENERAL
SEC. 407. (a) Whenever the Attorney General receives a complaint in writing—
(1) signed by a parent or group of parents to the effect that his or their minor children, as members of a class of persons similarly situated, are being deprived by a school board of the equal protection of the laws, or
(2) signed by an individual, or his parent, to the effect that he has been denied admission to or not permitted to continue in attendance at a public college by reason of race, color, religion, or national origin, and the Attorney General believes the complaint is meritorious and certifies that the signer or signers of such complaint are unable, in his judgment, to initiate and maintain appropriate legal proceedings for relief and that the institution of an action will materially further the orderly achievement of desegregation in public education, the Attorney General is authorized, after giving notice of such complaint to the appropriate school board or college authority and after certifying that he is satisfied that such board or authority has had a reasonable time to adjust the conditions alleged in such complaint, to institute for or in the name of the United States a civil action in any appropriate district court of the United States against such parties and for such relief as may be appropriate, and such court shall have and shall exercise jurisdiction of proceedings instituted pursuant to this section, provided that nothing herein shall empower any official or court of the United States to issue any order seeking to achieve a racial balance in any school by requiring the transportation of pupils or students from one school to another or one school district to another in order to achieve such racial balance, or otherwise enlarge the existing power of the court to insure compliance with constitutional standards. The Attorney General may implead as defendants such additional parties as are or become necessary to the grant of effective relief hereunder.
(b) The Attorney General may deem a person or persons unable to initiate and maintain appropriate legal proceedings within the meaning of subsection
(a) of this section when such person or persons are unable, either directly or through other interested persons or organizations, to bear the expense of the litigation or to obtain effective legal representation; or whenever he is satisfied that the institution of such litigation would jeopardize the personal safety, employment, or economic standing of such person or persons, their families, or their property.
(c) The term "parent" as used in this section includes any person standing in loco parentis. A "complaint" as used in this section is a writing or document within the meaning of section 1001, title 18, United States Code.
SEC. 408. In any action or proceeding under this title the United States

shall be liable for costs the same as a private person.
SEC. 409. Nothing in this title shall affect adversely the right of any person to sue for or obtain relief in any court against discrimination in public education.
SEC. 410. Nothing in this title shall prohibit classification and assignment for reasons other than race, color, religion, or national origin.

TITLE V—COMMISSION ON CIVIL RIGHTS
SEC. 501. Section 102 of the Civil Rights Act of 1957 (42 U.S.C. 1975a; 71 Stat. 634) is amended to read as follows:

"RULES OF PROCEDURE OF THE COMMISSION HEARINGS
"SEC. 102. (a) At least thirty days prior to the commencement of any hearing, the Commission shall cause to be published in the Federal Register notice of the date on which such hearing is to commence, the place at which it is to be held and the subject of the hearing. The Chairman, or one designated by him to act as Chairman at a hearing of the Commission, shall announce in an opening statement the subject of the hearing.
"(b) A copy of the Commission's rules shall be made available to any witness before the Commission, and a witness compelled to appear before the Commission or required to produce written or other matter shall be served with a copy of the Commission's rules at the time of service of the subpoena.
"(c) Any person compelled to appear in person before the Commission shall be accorded the right to be accompanied and advised by counsel, who shall have the right to subject his client to reasonable examination, and to make objections on the record and to argue briefly the basis for such objections. The Commission shall proceed with reasonable dispatch to conclude any hearing in which it is engaged. Due regard shall be had for the convenience and necessity of witnesses.
"(d) The Chairman or Acting Chairman may punish breaches of order and decorum by censure and exclusion from the hearings.
"(e) If the Commission determines that evidence or testimony at any hearing may tend to defame, degrade, or incriminate any person, it shall receive such evidence or testimony or summary of such evidence o testimony in executive session. The Commission shall afford any person defamed, degraded, or incriminated by such evidence or testimony an opportunity to appear and be heard in executive session, with a reasonable number of additional witnesses requested by him, before deciding to use such evidence or testimony. In the event the Commission determines to release or use such evidence or testimony in such manner as to reveal publicly the identity of the person defamed, degraded, or incriminated, such evidence or testimony, prior to such public release or use, shall be given at a public session, and the Commission shall afford such person an opportunity to appear as a voluntary witness or to file a sworn statement in his behalf and to submit brief and pertinent sworn statements of others. The Commission shall receive and dispose of requests from such person to subpoena additional witnesses.
"(f) Except as provided in sections 102 and 105 (f) of this Act, the Chairman shall receive and the Commission shall dispose of requests to

subpoena additional witnesses.

"(g) No evidence or testimony or summary of evidence or testimony taken in executive session may be released or used in public sessions without the consent of the Commission. Whoever releases or uses in public without the consent of the Commission such evidence or testimony taken in executive session shall be fined not more than $1,000, or imprisoned for not more than one year.

"(h) In the discretion of the Commission, witnesses may submit brief and pertinent sworn statements in writing for inclusion in the record. The Commission shall determine the pertinency of testimony and evidence adduced at its hearings.

"(i) Every person who submits data or evidence shall be entitled to retain or, on payment of lawfully prescribed costs, procure a copy or transcript thereof, except that a witness in a hearing held in executive session may for good cause be limited to inspection of the official transcript of his testimony. Transcript copies of public sessions may be obtained by the public upon the payment of the cost thereof. An accurate transcript shall be made of the testimony of all witnesses at all hearings, either public or executive sessions, of the Commission or of any subcommittee thereof.

"(j) A witness attending any session of the Commission shall receive $6 for each day's attendance and for the time necessarily occupied in going to and returning from the same, and 10 cents per mile for going from and returning to his place of residence. Witnesses who attend at points so far removed from their respective residences as to prohibit return thereto from day to day shall be entitled to an additional allowance of $10 per day for expenses of subsistence including the time necessarily occupied in going to and returning from the place of attendance. Mileage payments shall be tendered to the witness upon service of a subpoena issued on behalf of the Commission or any subcommittee thereof.

"(k) The Commission shall not issue any subpoena for the attendance and testimony of witnesses or for the production of written or other matter which would require the presence of the party subpoenaed at a hearing to be held outside of the State wherein the witness is found or resides or is domiciled or transacts business, or has appointed an agent for receipt of service of process except that, in any event, the Commission may issue subpoenas for the attendance and testimony of witnesses and the production of written or other matter at a hearing held within fifty miles of the place where the witness is found or resides or is domiciled or transacts business or has appointed an agent for receipt of service of process.

"(l) The Commission shall separately state and currently publish in the Federal Register (1) descriptions of its central and field organization including the established places at which, and methods whereby, the public may secure information or make requests; (2) statements of the general course and method by which its functions are channeled and determined, and (3) rules adopted as authorized by law. No person shall in any manner be subject to or required to resort to rules, organization, or procedure not so published."

SEC. 502. Section 103(a) of the Civil Rights Act of 1957 (42 U.S.C. 1975b(a); 71 Stat. 634) is amended to read as follows:

"SEC. 103. (a) Each member of the Commission who is not otherwise in the service of the Government of the United States shall receive the sum of $75 per day for each day spent in the work of the Commission, shall be paid actual travel expenses, and per diem in lieu of subsistence expenses when away from his usual place of residence, in accordance with section 5 of the Administrative Expenses Act of 1946, as amended (5 U.S.C 73b-2; 60 Stat. 808)."

SEC. 503. Section 103(b) of the Civil Rights Act of 1957 (42 U.S.C. 1975(b); 71 Stat. 634) is amended to read as follows:

"(b) Each member of the Commission who is otherwise in the service of the Government of the United States shall serve without compensation in addition to that received for such other service, but while engaged in the work of the Commission shall be paid actual travel expenses, and per diem in lieu of subsistence expenses when away from his usual place of residence, in accordance with the provisions of the Travel Expenses Act of 1949, as amended
(5 U.S.C. 835-42; 63 Stat. 166)."

SEC. 504. (a) Section 104(a) of the Civil Rights Act of 1957 (42 U.S.C. 1975c(a); 71 Stat. 635), as amended, is further amended to read as follows:

"DUTIES OF THE COMMISSION

"SEC. 104. (a) The Commission shall—

"(1) investigate allegations in writing under oath or affirmation that certain citizens of the United States are being deprived of their right to vote and have that vote counted by reason of their color, race, religion, or national origin; which writing, under oath or affirmation, shall set forth the facts upon which such belief or beliefs are based;

"(2) study and collect information concerning legal developments constituting a denial of equal protection of the laws under the Constitution because of race, color, religion or national origin or in the administration of justice;

"(3) appraise the laws and policies of the Federal Government with respect to denials of equal protection of the laws under the Constitution because of race, color, religion or national origin or in the administration of justice;

"(4) serve as a national clearinghouse for information in respect to denials of equal protection of the laws because of race, color, religion or national origin, including but not limited to the fields of voting, education, housing, employment, the use of public facilities, and transportation, or in the administration of justice;

"(5) investigate allegations, made in writing and under oath or affirmation, that citizens of the United States are unlawfully being accorded or denied the right to vote, or to have their votes properly counted, in any election of presidential electors, Members of the United States Senate, or of the House of Representatives, as a result of any patterns or practice of fraud or discrimination in the conduct of such election; and

"(6) Nothing in this or any other Act shall be construed as authorizing the Commission, its Advisory Committees, or any person under its supervision or control to inquire into or investigate any membership practices or internal operations of any fraternal organization, any college or university fraternity or sorority, any private club or any religious organization."

(b) Section 104(b) of the Civil Rights Act of 1957 (42 U.S.C. 1975c(b); 71

Stat. 635), as amended, is further amended by striking out the present subsection "(b)" and by substituting therefor:

"(b) The Commission shall submit interim reports to the President and to the Congress at such times as the Commission, the Congress or the President shall deem desirable, and shall submit to the President and to the Congress a final report of its activities, findings, and recommendations not later than January 31, 1968."

SEC. 505. Section 105(a) of the Civil Rights Act of 1957 (42 U.S.C. 1975d(a); 71 Stat. 636) is amended by striking out in the last sentence thereof "$50 per diem" and inserting in lieu thereof "$75 per diem."

SEC. 506. Section 105(f) and section 105(g) of the Civil Rights Act of 1957 (42 U.S.C. 1975d (f) and (g); 71 Stat. 636) are amended to read as follows:

"(f) The Commission, or on the authorization of the Commission any subcommittee of two or more members, at least one of whom shall be of each major political party, may, for the purpose of carrying out the provisions of this Act, hold such hearings and act at such times and places as the Commission or such authorized subcommittee may deem advisable. Subpoenas for the attendance and testimony of witnesses or the production of written or other matter may be issued in accordance with the rules of the Commission as contained in section 102 (j) and (k) of this Act, over the signature of the Chairman of the Commission or of such subcommittee, and may be served by any person designated by such Chairman. The holding of hearings by the Commission, or the appointment of a subcommittee to hold hearings pursuant to this subparagraph, must be approved by a majority of the Commission, or by a majority of the members present at a meeting at which at least a quorum of four members is present.

"(g) In case of contumacy or refusal to obey a subpoena, any district court of the United States or the United States court of any territory or possession, or the District Court of the United States for the District of Columbia, within the jurisdiction of which the inquiry is carried on or within the jurisdiction of which said person guilty of contumacy or refusal to obey is found or resides or is domiciled or transacts business, or has appointed an agent for receipt of service of process, upon application by the Attorney General of the United States shall have jurisdiction to issue to such person an order requiring such person to appear before the Commission or a subcommittee thereof, there to produce pertinent, relevant and nonprivileged evidence if so ordered, or there to give testimony touching the matter under investigation; and any failure to obey such order of the court may be punished by said court as a contempt thereof."

SEC. 507. Section 105 of the Civil Rights Act of 1957 (42 U.S.C. 1975d; 71 Stat. 636), as amended by section 401 of the Civil Rights Act of 1960 (42 U.S.C. 1975d(h); 74 Stat. 89), is further amended by adding a new subsection at the end to read as follows:

"(i) The Commission shall have the power to make such rules and regulations as are necessary to carry out the purposes of this Act."

TITLE VI—NONDISCRIMINATION IN FEDERALLY ASSISTED PROGRAMS

SEC. 601. No person in the United States shall, on the ground of race, color, or national origin, be excluded from participation in, be denied the benefits of, or be subjected to discrimination under any program or activity receiving Federal financial assistance.

SEC. 602. Each Federal department and agency which is empowered to extend Federal financial assistance to any program or activity, by way of grant, loan, or contract other than a contract of insurance or guaranty, is authorized and directed to effectuate the provisions of section 601 with respect to such program or activity by issuing rules, regulations, or orders of general applicability which shall be consistent with achievement of the objectives of the statute authorizing the financial assistance in connection with which the action is taken. No such rule, regulation, or order shall become effective unless and until approved by the President. Compliance with any requirement adopted pursuant to this section may be effected (1) by the termination of or refusal to grant or to continue assistance under such program or activity to any recipient as to whom there has been an express finding on the record, after opportunity for hearing, of a failure to comply with such requirement, but such termination or refusal shall be limited to the particular political entity, or part thereof, or other recipient as to whom such a finding has been made and, shall be limited in its effect to the particular program, or part thereof, in which such non-compliance has been so found, or (2) by any other means authorized by law: Provided, however, That no such action shall be taken until the department or agency concerned has advised the appropriate person or persons of the failure to comply with the requirement and has determined that compliance cannot be secured by voluntary means. In the case of any action terminating, or refusing to grant or continue, assistance because of failure to comply with a requirement imposed pursuant to this section, the head of the federal department or agency shall file with the committees of the House and Senate having legislative jurisdiction over the program or activity involved a full written report of the circumstances and the grounds for such action. No such action shall become effective until thirty days have elapsed after the filing of such report.

SEC. 603. Any department or agency action taken pursuant to section 602 shall be subject to such judicial review as may otherwise be provided by law for similar action taken by such department or agency on other grounds. In the case of action, not otherwise subject to judicial review, terminating or refusing to grant or to continue financial assistance upon a finding of failure to comply with any requirement imposed pursuant to section 602, any person aggrieved (including any State or political subdivision thereof and any agency of either) may obtain judicial review of such action in accordance with section 10 of the Administrative Procedure Act, and such action shall not be deemed committed to unreviewable agency discretion within the meaning of that section.

SEC. 604. Nothing contained in this title shall be construed to authorize action under this title by any department or agency with respect to any employment practice of any employer, employment agency, or labor organization except where a primary objective of the Federal financial assistance is to provide employment.

SEC. 605. Nothing in this title shall add to or detract from any existing authority with respect to any program or activity under which Federal financial assistance is extended by way of a contract of insurance or guaranty.

TITLE VII—EQUAL EMPLOYMENT OPPORTUNITY DEFINITIONS
SEC. 701. For the purposes of this title—
(a) The term "person" includes one or more individuals, labor unions, partnerships, associations, corporations, legal representatives, mutual companies, joint-stock companies, trusts, unincorporated organizations, trustees, trustees in bankruptcy, or receivers.
(b) The term "employer" means a person engaged in an industry affecting commerce who has twenty-five or more employees for each working day in each of twenty or more calendar weeks in the current or preceding calendar year, and any agent of such a person, but such term does not include (1) the United States, a corporation wholly owned by the Government of the United States, an Indian tribe, or a State or political subdivision thereof, (2) a bona fide private membership club (other than a labor organization) which is exempt from taxation under section 501(c) of the Internal Revenue Code of 1954: Provided, That during the first year after the effective date prescribed in subsection (a) of section 716, persons having fewer than one hundred employees (and their agents) shall not be considered employers, and, during the second year after such date, persons having fewer than seventy-five employees (and their agents) shall not be considered employers, and, during the third year after such date, persons having fewer than fifty employees (and their agents) shall not be considered employers: Provided further, That it shall be the policy of the United States to insure equal employment opportunities for Federal employees without discrimination because of race, color, religion, sex or national origin and the President shall utilize his existing authority to effectuate this policy.
(c) The term "employment agency" means any person regularly undertaking with or without compensation to procure employees for an employer or to procure for employees opportunities to work for an employer and includes an agent of such a person; but shall not include an agency of the United States, or an agency of a State or political subdivision of a State, except that such term shall include the United States Employment Service and the system of State and local employment services receiving Federal assistance.
(d) The term "labor organization" means a labor organization engaged in an industry affecting commerce, and any agent of such an organization, and includes any organization of any kind, any agency, or employee representation committee, group, association, or plan so engaged in which employees participate and which exists for the purpose, in whole or in part, of dealing with employers concerning grievances, labor disputes, wages, rates of pay, hours, or other terms or conditions of employment, and any conference, general committee, joint or system board, or joint council so engaged which is subordinate to a national or international labor organization.
(e) A labor organization shall be deemed to be engaged in an industry affecting commerce if (1) it maintains or operates a hiring hall or hiring office which procures employees for an employer or procures for employees opportunities to work for an employer, or (2) the number of its members (or, where it is a labor organization composed of other labor organizations or their representatives, if the aggregate number of the members of such other labor organization) is (A) one hundred or more

during the first year after the effective date prescribed in subsection (a) of section 716, (B) seventy-five or more during the second year after such date or fifty or more during the third year, or (C) twenty-five or more thereafter, and such labor organization—

(1) is the certified representative of employees under the provisions of the National Labor Relations Act, as amended, or the Railway Labor Act, as amended;

(2) although not certified, is a national or international labor organization or a local labor organization recognized or acting as the representative of employees of an employer or employers engaged in an industry affecting commerce; or

(3) has chartered a local labor organization or subsidiary body which is representing or actively seeking to represent employees of employers within the meaning of paragraph (1) or (2); or

(4) has been chartered by a labor organization representing or actively seeking to represent employees within the meaning of paragraph (1) or (2) as the local or subordinate body through which such employees may enjoy membership or become affiliated with such labor organization; or

(5) is a conference, general committee, joint or system board, or joint council subordinate to a national or international labor organization, which includes a labor organization engaged in an industry affecting commerce within the meaning of any of the preceding paragraphs of this subsection.

(f) The term "employee" means an individual employed by an employer.

(g) The term "commerce" means trade, traffic, commerce, transportation, transmission, or communication among the several States; or between a State and any place outside thereof; or within the District of Columbia, or a possession of the United States; or between points in the same State but through a point outside thereof.

(h) The term "industry affecting commerce" means any activity, business, or industry in commerce or in which a labor dispute would hinder or obstruct commerce or the free flow of commerce and includes any activity or industry "affecting commerce" within the meaning of the Labor-Management Reporting and Disclosure Act of 1959.

(i) The term "State" includes a State of the United States, the District of Columbia, Puerto Rico, the Virgin Islands, American Samoa, Guam, Wake Island, The Canal Zone, and Outer Continental Shelf lands defined in the Outer Continental Shelf Lands Act.

EXEMPTION

SEC. 702. This title shall not apply to an employer with respect to the employment of aliens outside any State, or to a religious corporation, association, or society with respect to the employment of individuals of a particular religion to perform work connected with the carrying on by such corporation, association, or society of its religious activities or to an educational institution with respect to the employment of individuals to perform work connected with the educational activities of such institution.

DISCRIMINATION BECAUSE OF RACE, COLOR, RELIGION, SEX, OR NATIONAL ORIGIN

SEC. 703. (a) It shall be an unlawful employment practice for an employer—

(1) to fail or refuse to hire or to discharge any individual, or otherwise to discriminate against any individual with respect to his compensation, terms, conditions, or privileges of employment, because of such individual's race, color, religion, sex, or national origin; or

(2) to limit, segregate, or classify his employees in any way which would deprive or tend to deprive any individual of employment opportunities or otherwise adversely affect his status as an employee, because of such individual's race, color, religion, sex, or national origin.

(b) It shall be an unlawful employment practice for an employment agency to fail or refuse to refer for employment, or otherwise to discriminate against, any individual because of his race, color, religion, sex, or national origin, or to classify or refer for employment any individual on the basis of his race, color, religion, sex, or national origin.

(c) It shall be an unlawful employment practice for a labor organization—

(1) to exclude or to expel from its membership, or otherwise to discriminate against, any individual because of his race, color, religion, sex, or national origin;

(2) to limit, segregate, or classify its membership, or to classify or fail or refuse to refer for employment any individual, in any way which would deprive or tend to deprive any individual of employment opportunities, or would limit such employment opportunities or otherwise adversely affect his status as an employee or as an applicant for employment, because of such individual's race, color, religion, sex, or national origin; or

(3) to cause or attempt to cause an employer to discriminate against an individual in violation of this section.

(d) It shall be an unlawful employment practice for any employer, labor organization, or joint labor-management committee controlling apprenticeship or other training or retraining, including on-the-job training programs to discriminate against any individual because of his race, color, religion, sex, or national origin in admission to, or employment in, any program established to provide apprenticeship or other training.

(e) Notwithstanding any other provision of this title, (1) it shall not be an unlawful employment practice for an employer to hire and employ employees, for an employment agency to classify, or refer for employment any individual, for a labor organization to classify its membership or to classify or refer for employment any individual, or for an employer, labor organization, or joint labor-management committee controlling apprenticeship or other training or retraining programs to admit or employ any individual in any such program, on the basis of his religion, sex, or national origin in those certain instances where religion, sex, or national origin is a bona fide occupational qualification reasonably necessary to the normal operation of that particular business or enterprise, and (2) it shall not be an unlawful employment practice for a school, college, university, or other educational institution or institution of learning to hire and employ employees of a particular religion if such school, college, university, or other educational *institution or institution of learning is, in whole or in substantial part, owned, supported, controlled, or managed by a particular religion or by a particular religious corporation, association, or society, or if the curriculum of such school, college, university, or other educational institution or institution of learning is directed toward the propagation of a particular religion.*

(f) As used in this title, the phrase "unlawful employment practice" shall not be deemed to include any action or measure taken by an employer, labor organization, joint labor-management committee, or employment agency with respect to an individual who is a member of the Communist Party of the United States or of any other organization required to register as a Communist-action or Communist-front organization by final order of the Subversive Activities Control Board pursuant to the Subversive Activities Control Act of 1950.

(g) Notwithstanding any other provision of this title, it shall not be an unlawful employment practice for an employer to fail or refuse to hire and employ any individual for any position, for an employer to discharge any individual from any position, or for an employment agency to fail or refuse to refer any individual for employment in any position, or for a labor organization to fail or refuse to refer any individual for employment in any position, if—

(1) the occupancy of such position, or access to the premises in or upon which any part of the duties of such position is performed or is to be performed, is subject to any requirement imposed in the interest of the national security of the United States under any security program in effect pursuant to or administered under any statute of the United States or any Executive order of the President; and

(2) such individual has not fulfilled or has ceased to fulfill that requirement.

(h) Notwithstanding any other provision of this title, it shall not be an unlawful employment practice for an employer to apply different standards of compensation, or different terms, conditions, or privileges of employment pursuant to a bona fide seniority or merit system, or a system which measures earnings by quantity or quality of production or to employees who work in different locations, provided that such differences are not the result of an intention to discriminate because of race, color, religion, sex, or national origin, nor shall it be an unlawful employment practice for an employer to give and to act upon the results of any professionally developed ability test provided that such test, its administration or action upon the results is not designed, intended or used to discriminate because of race, color, religion, sex or national origin. It shall not be an unlawful employment practice under this title for any employer to differentiate upon the basis of sex in determining the amount of the wages or compensation paid or to be paid to employees of such employer if such differentiation is authorized by the provisions of section 6(d) of the Fair Labor Standards Act of 1938, as amended (29 U.S.C. 206(d)).

(i) Nothing contained in this title shall apply to any business or enterprise on or near an Indian reservation with respect to any publicly announced employment practice of such business or enterprise under which a preferential treatment is given to any individual because he is an Indian living on or near a reservation.

(j) Nothing contained in this title shall be interpreted to require any employer, employment agency, labor organization, or joint labor-management committee subject to this title to grant preferential treatment to any individual or to any group because of the race, color, religion, sex, or national origin of such individual or group on account of an imbalance which may exist with respect to the total number or percentage of persons of any race, color, religion, sex, or national origin employed by an employer, referred or classified for employment by any employment agency or labor organization, admitted to membership or classified by any labor organization, or admitted to, or employed in, any apprenticeship or other training program, in comparison with the total number or percentage of persons of such race, color, religion, sex, or national origin in any community, State, section, or other area, or in the available work force in any community, State, section, or other area.

OTHER UNLAWFUL EMPLOYMENT PRACTICES
SEC. 704. (a) It shall be an unlawful employment practice for an employer to discriminate against any of his employees or applicants for employment, for an employment agency to discriminate against any individual, or for a labor organization to discriminate against any member thereof or applicant for membership, because he has opposed, any practice made an unlawful employment practice by this title, or because he has made a charge, testified, assisted, or participated in any manner in an investigation, proceeding, or hearing under this title.
(b) It shall be an unlawful employment practice for an employer, labor organization, or employment agency to print or publish or cause to be printed or published any notice or advertisement relating to employment by such an employer or membership in or any classification or referral for employment by such a labor organization, or relating to any classification or referral for employment by such an employment agency, indicating any preference, limitation, specification, or discrimination, based on race, color, religion, sex, or national origin, except that such a notice or advertisement may indicate a preference, limitation, specification, or discrimination based on religion, sex, or national origin when religion, sex, or national origin is a bona fide occupational qualification for employment.

EQUAL EMPLOYMENT OPPORTUNITY COMMISSION
SEC. 705. (a) There is hereby created a Commission to be known as the Equal Employment Opportunity Commission, which shall be composed of five members, not more than three of whom shall be members of the same political party, who shall be appointed by the President by and with the advice and consent of the Senate. One of the original members shall be appointed for a term of one year, one for a term of two years, one for a term of three years, one for a term of four years, and one for a term of five years, beginning from the date of enactment of this title, but their successors shall be appointed for terms of five years each, except that any individual chosen to fill a vacancy shall be appointed only for the unexpired term of the member whom he shall succeed. The President shall designate one member to serve as Chairman of the Commission, and one member to serve as Vice Chairman. The Chairman shall be responsible on behalf of the Commission for the administrative operations of the

Commission, and shall appoint, in accordance with the civil service laws, such officers, agents, attorneys, and employees as it deems necessary to assist it in the performance of its functions and to fix their compensation in accordance with the Classification Act of 1949, as amended. The Vice Chairman shall act as Chairman in the absence or disability of the Chairman or in the event of a vacancy in that office.
(b) A vacancy in the Commission shall not impair the right of the remaining members to exercise all the powers of the Commission and three members thereof shall constitute a quorum.
(c) The Commission shall have an official seal which shall be judicially noticed.
(d) The Commission shall at the close of each fiscal year report to the Congress and to the President concerning the action it has taken; the names, salaries, and duties of all individuals in its employ and the moneys it has disbursed; and shall make such further reports on the cause of and means of eliminating discrimination and such recommendations for further legislation as may appear desirable.
(e) The Federal Executive Pay Act of 1956, as amended (5 U.S.C. 2201-2209), is further amended—
(1) by adding to section 105 thereof (5 U.S.C. 2204) the following clause: "(32) Chairman, Equal Employment Opportunity Commission"; and
(2) by adding to clause (45) of section 106(a) thereof (5 U.S.C. 2205(a)) the following: "Equal Employment Opportunity Commission (4)."
(f) The principal office of the Commission shall be in or near the District of Columbia, but it may meet or exercise any or all its powers at any other place. The Commission may establish such regional or State offices as it deems necessary to accomplish the purpose of this title.
(g) The Commission shall have power—
(1) to cooperate with and, with their consent, utilize regional, State, local, and other agencies, both public and private, and individuals;
(2) to pay to witnesses whose depositions are taken or who are summoned before the Commission or any of its agents the same witness and mileage fees as are paid to witnesses in the courts of the United States;
(3) to furnish to persons subject to this title such technical assistance as they may request to further their compliance with this title or an order issued thereunder;
(4) upon the request of (i) any employer, whose employees or some of them, or (ii) any labor organization, whose members or some of them, refuse or threaten to refuse to cooperate in effectuating the provisions of this title, to assist in such effectuation by conciliation or such other remedial action as is provided by this title;
(5) to make such technical studies as are appropriate to effectuate the purposes and policies of this title and to make the results of such studies available to the public;
(6) to refer matters to the Attorney General with recommendations for intervention in a civil action brought by an aggrieved party under section 706, or for the institution of a civil action by the Attorney General under section 707, and to advise, consult, and assist the Attorney General on such matters.
(h) Attorneys appointed under this section may, at the direction of the Commission, appear for and represent the Commission in any case in court.
(i) The Commission shall, in any of its educational or promotional

activities, cooperate with other departments and agencies in the performance of such educational and promotional activities.
(j) All officers, agents, attorneys, and employees of the Commission shall be subject to the provisions of section 9 of the Act of August 2, 1939, as amended (the Hatch Act), notwithstanding any exemption contained in such section.

PREVENTION OF UNLAWFUL EMPLOYMENT PRACTICES
SEC. 706. (a) Whenever it is charged in writing under oath by a person claiming to be aggrieved, or a written charge has been filed by a member of the Commission where he has reasonable cause to believe a violation of this title has occurred (and such charge sets forth the facts upon which it is based) that an employer, employment agency, or labor organization has engaged in an unlawful employment practice, the Commission shall furnish such employer, employment agency, or labor organization (hereinafter referred to as the "respondent") with a copy of such charge and shall make an investigation of such charge, provided that such charge shall not be made public by the Commission. If the Commission shall determine, after such investigation, that there is reasonable cause to believe that the charge is true, the Commission shall endeavor to eliminate any such alleged unlawful employment practice by informal methods of conference, conciliation, and persuasion. Nothing said or done during and as a part of such endeavors may be made public by the Commission without the written consent of the parties, or used as evidence in a subsequent proceeding. Any officer or employee of the Commission, who shall make public in any manner whatever any information in violation of this subsection shall be deemed guilty of a misdemeanor and upon conviction thereof shall be fined not more than $1,000 or imprisoned not more than one year.
(b) In the case of an alleged unlawful employment practice occurring in a State, or political subdivision of a State, which has a State or local law prohibiting the unlawful employment practice alleged and establishing or authorizing a State or local authority to grant or seek relief from such practice or to institute criminal proceedings with respect thereto upon receiving notice thereof, no charge may be filed under subsection (a) by the person aggrieved before the expiration of sixty days after proceedings have been commenced under the State or local law, unless such proceedings have been earlier terminated, provided that such sixty-day period shall be extended to one hundred and twenty days during the first year after the effective date of such State or local law. If any requirement for the commencement of such proceedings is imposed by a State or local authority other than a requirement of the filing of a written and signed statement of the facts upon which the proceeding is based, the proceeding shall be deemed to have been commenced for the purposes of this subsection at the time such statement is sent by registered mail to the appropriate State or local authority.
(c) In the case of any charge filed by a member of the Commission alleging an unlawful employment practice occurring in a State or political subdivision of a State, which has a State or local law prohibiting the practice alleged and establishing or authorizing a State or local authority to grant or seek relief from such practice or to institute criminal proceedings with respect thereto upon receiving notice thereof,

the Commission shall, before taking any action with respect to such charge, notify the appropriate State or local officials and, upon request, afford them a reasonable time, but not less than sixty days (provided that such sixty-day period shall be extended to one hundred and twenty days during the first year after the effective day of such State or local law), unless a shorter period is requested, to act under such State or local law to remedy the practice alleged.

(d) A charge under subsection (a) shall be filed within ninety days after the alleged unlawful employment practice occurred, except that in the case of an unlawful employment practice with respect to which the person aggrieved has followed the procedure set out in subsection (b), such charge shall be filed by the person aggrieved within two hundred and ten days after the alleged unlawful employment practice occurred, or within thirty days after receiving notice that the State or local agency has terminated the proceedings under the State or local, law, whichever is earlier, and a copy of such charge shall be filed by the Commission with the State or local agency.

(e) If within thirty days after a charge is filed with the Commission or within thirty days after expiration of any period of reference under subsection (c) (except that in either case such period may be extended to not more than sixty days upon a determination by the Commission that further efforts to secure voluntary compliance are warranted), the Commission has been unable to obtain voluntary compliance with this title, the Commission shall so notify the person aggrieved and a civil action may, within thirty days thereafter, be brought against the respondent named in the charge (1) by the person claiming to be aggrieved, or (2) if such charge was filed by a member of the Commission, by any person whom the charge alleges was aggrieved by the alleged unlawful employment practice. Upon application by the complainant and in such circumstances as the court may deem just, the court may appoint an attorney for such complainant and may authorize the commencement of the action without the payment of fees, costs, or security. Upon timely application, the court may, in its discretion, permit the Attorney General to intervene in such civil action if he certifies that the case is of general public importance. Upon request, the court may, in its discretion, stay further proceedings for not more than sixty days pending the termination of State or local proceedings described in subsection (b) or the efforts of the Commission to obtain voluntary compliance.

(f) Each United States district court and each United States court of a place subject to the jurisdiction of the United States shall have jurisdiction of actions brought under this title. Such an action may be brought in any judicial district in the State in which the unlawful employment practice is alleged to have been committed, in the judicial district in which the employment records relevant to such practice are maintained and administered, or in the judicial district in which the plaintiff would have worked but for the alleged unlawful employment practice, but if the respondent is not found within any such district, such an action may be brought within the judicial district in which the respondent has his principal office. For purposes of sections 1404 and 1406 of title 28 of the United States Code, the judicial district in which the respondent has his principal office shall in all cases be considered a district in which the action might have been brought.

(g) If the court finds that the respondent has intentionally engaged in or is intentionally engaging in an unlawful employment practice charged in the complaint, the court may enjoin the respondent from engaging in such unlawful employment practice, and order such affirmative action as may be appropriate, which may include reinstatement or hiring of employees, with or without back pay (payable by the employer, employment agency, or labor organization, as the case may be, responsible for the unlawful employment practice). Interim earnings or amounts earnable with reasonable diligence by the person or persons discriminated against shall operate to reduce the back pay otherwise allowable. No order of the court shall require the admission or reinstatement of an individual as a member of a union or the hiring, reinstatement, or promotion of an individual as an employee, or the payment to him of any back pay, if such individual was refused admission, suspended, or expelled or was refused employment or advancement or was suspended or discharged for any reason other than discrimination on account of race, color, religion, sex or national origin or in violation of section 704(a).

(h) The provisions of the Act entitled "An Act to amend the Judicial Code and to define and limit the jurisdiction of courts sitting in equity, and for other purposes," approved March 23, 1932 (29 U.S.C. 101-115), shall not apply with respect to civil actions brought under this section.

(i) In any case in which an employer, employment agency, or labor organization fails to comply with an order of a court issued in a civil action brought under subsection (e), the Commission may commence proceedings to compel compliance with such order.

(j) Any civil action brought under subsection (e) and any proceedings brought under subsection (i) shall be subject to appeal as provided in sections 1291 and 1292, title 28, United States Code.

(k) In any action or proceeding under this title the court, in its discretion, may allow the prevailing party, other than the Commission or the United States, a reasonable attorney's fee as part of the costs, and the Commission and the United States shall be liable for costs the same as a private person.

SEC. 707. (a) Whenever the Attorney General has reasonable cause to believe that any person or group of persons is engaged in a pattern or practice of resistance to the full enjoyment of any of the rights secured by this title, and that the pattern or practice is of such a nature and is intended to deny the full exercise of the rights herein described, the Attorney General may bring a civil action in the appropriate district court of the United States by filing with it a complaint (1) signed by him (or in his absence the Acting Attorney General), (2) setting forth facts pertaining to such pattern or practice, and (3) requesting such relief, including an application for a permanent or temporary injunction, restraining order or other order against the person or persons responsible for such pattern or practice, as he deems necessary to insure the full enjoyment of the rights herein described.

(b) The district courts of the United States shall have and shall exercise jurisdiction of proceedings instituted pursuant to this section, and in any such proceeding the Attorney General may file with the clerk of such court a request that a court of three judges be convened to hear and determine the case. Such request by the Attorney General shall be

accompanied by a certificate that, in his opinion, the case is of general
public importance. A copy of the certificate and request for a three-judge
court shall be immediately furnished by such clerk to the chief judge of
the circuit (or in his absence, the presiding circuit judge of the
circuit) in which the case is pending. Upon receipt of such request it
shall be the duty of the chief judge of the circuit or the presiding
circuit judge, as the case may be, to designate immediately three judges
in such circuit, of whom at least one shall be a circuit judge and another
of whom shall be a district judge of the court in which the proceeding was
instituted, to hear and determine such case, and it shall be the duty of
the judges so designated to assign the case for hearing at the earliest
practicable date, to participate in the hearing and determination thereof,
and to cause the case to be in every way expedited. An appeal from the
final judgment of such court will lie to the Supreme Court.
In the event the Attorney General fails to file such a request in any such
proceeding, it shall be the duty of the chief judge of the district (or in
his absence, the acting chief judge) in which the case is pending
immediately to designate a judge in such district to hear and determine
the case. In the event that no judge in the district is available to hear
and determine the case, the chief judge of the district, or the acting
chief judge, as the case may be, shall certify this fact to the chief
judge of the circuit (or in his absence, the acting chief judge) who shall
then designate a district or circuit judge of the circuit to hear and
determine the case.
It shall be the duty of the judge designated pursuant to this section to
assign the case for hearing at the earliest practicable date and to cause
the case to be in every way expedited.

EFFECT ON STATE LAWS
SEC. 708. Nothing in this title shall be deemed to exempt or relieve any
person from any liability, duty, penalty, or punishment provided by any
present or future law of any State or political subdivision of a State,
other than any such law which purports to require or permit the doing of
any act which would be an unlawful employment practice under this title.

INVESTIGATIONS, INSPECTIONS, RECORDS, STATE AGENCIES
SEC. 709. (a) In connection with any investigation of a charge filed under
section 706, the Commission or its designated representative shall at all
reasonable times have access to, for the purposes of examination, and the
right to copy any evidence of any person being investigated or proceeded
against that relates to unlawful employment practices covered by this
title and is relevant to the charge under investigation.
(b) The Commission may cooperate with State and local agencies charged
with the administration of State fair employment practices laws and, with
the consent of such agencies, may for the purpose of carrying out its
functions and duties under this title and within the limitation of funds
appropriated specifically for such purpose, utilize the services of such
agencies and their employees and, notwithstanding any other provision of
law, may reimburse such agencies and their employees for services rendered
to assist the Commission in carrying out this title. In furtherance of
such cooperative efforts, the Commission may enter into written agreements
with such State or local agencies and such agreements may include

provisions under which the Commission shall refrain from processing a charge in any cases or class of cases specified in such agreements and under which no person may bring a civil action under section 706 in any cases or class of cases so specified, or under which the Commission shall relieve any person or class of persons in such State or locality from requirements imposed under this section. The Commission shall rescind any such agreement whenever it determines that the agreement no longer serves the interest of effective enforcement of this title.

(c) Except as provided in subsection (d), every employer, employment agency, and labor organization subject to this title shall (1) make and keep such records relevant to the determinations of whether unlawful employment practices have been or are being committed, (2) preserve such records for such periods, and (3) make such reports therefrom, as the Commission shall prescribe by regulation or order, after public hearing, as reasonable, necessary, or appropriate for the enforcement of this title or the regulations or orders thereunder. The Commission shall, by regulation, require each employer, labor organization, and joint labor-management committee subject to this title which controls an apprenticeship or other training program to maintain such records as are reasonably necessary to carry out the purpose of this title, including, but not limited to, a list of applicants who wish to participate in such program, including the chronological order in which such applications were received, and shall furnish to the Commission, upon request, a detailed description of the manner in which persons are selected to participate in the apprenticeship or other training program. Any employer, employment agency, labor organization, or joint labor-management committee which believes that the application to it of any regulation or order issued under this section would result in undue hardship may (1) apply to the Commission for an exemption from the application of such regulation or order, or (2) bring a civil action in the United States district court for the district where such records are kept. If the Commission or the court, as the case may be, finds that the application of the regulation or order to the employer, employment agency, or labor organization in question would impose an undue hardship, the Commission or the court, as the case may be, may grant appropriate relief.

(d) The provisions of subsection (c) shall not apply to any employer, employment agency, labor organization, or joint labor-management committee with respect to matters occurring in any State or political subdivision thereof which has a fair employment practice law during any period in which such employer, employment agency, labor organization, or joint labor-management committee is subject to such law, except that the Commission may require such notations on records which such employer, employment agency, labor organization, or joint labor-management committee keeps or is required to keep as are necessary because of differences in coverage or methods of enforcement between the State or local law and the provisions of this title. Where an employer is required by Executive Order 10925, issued March 6, 1961, or by any other Executive order prescribing fair employment practices for Government contractors and subcontractors, or by rules or regulations issued thereunder, to file reports relating to his employment practices with any Federal agency or committee, and he is

substantially in compliance with such requirements, the Commission shall not require him to file additional reports pursuant to subsection (c) of this section.
(e) It shall be unlawful for any officer or employee of the Commission to make public in any manner whatever any information obtained by the Commission pursuant to its authority under this section prior to the institution of any proceeding under this title involving such information. Any officer or employee of the Commission who shall make public in any manner whatever any information in violation of this subsection shall be guilty of a misdemeanor and upon conviction thereof, shall be fined not more than $1,000, or imprisoned not more than one year.

INVESTIGATORY POWERS
SEC. 710. (a) For the purposes of any investigation of a charge filed under the authority contained in section 706, the Commission shall have authority to examine witnesses under oath and to require the production of documentary evidence relevant or material to the charge under investigation.
(b) If the respondent named in a charge filed under section 706 fails or refuses to comply with a demand of the Commission for permission to examine or to copy evidence in conformity with the provisions of section 709(a), or if any person required to comply with the provisions of section 709 (c) or (d) fails or refuses to do so, or if any person fails or refuses to comply with a demand by the Commission to give testimony under oath, the United States district court for the district in which such person is found, resides, or transacts business, shall, upon application of the Commission, have jurisdiction to issue to such person an order requiring him to comply with the provisions of section 709 (c) or (d) or to comply with the demand of the Commission, but the attendance of a witness may not be required outside the State where he is found, resides, or transacts business and the production of evidence may not be required outside the State where such evidence is kept.
(c) Within twenty days after the service upon any person charged under section 706 of a demand by the Commission for the production of documentary evidence or for permission to examine or to copy evidence in conformity with the provisions of section 709(a), such person may file in the district court of the United States for the judicial district in which he resides, is found, or transacts business, and serve upon the Commission a petition for an order of such court modifying or setting aside such demand. The time allowed for compliance with the demand in whole or in part as deemed proper and ordered by the court shall not run during the pendency of such petition in the court. Such petition shall specify each ground upon which the petitioner relies in seeking such relief, and may be based upon any failure of such demand to comply with the provisions of this title or with the limitations generally applicable to compulsory process or upon any constitutional or other legal right or privilege of such person. No objection which is not raised by such a petition may be urged in the defense to a proceeding initiated by the Commission under subsection (b) for enforcement of such a demand unless such proceeding is commenced by the Commission prior to the expiration of the twenty-day period, or unless the court determines that the defendant could not

reasonably have been aware of the availability of such ground of objection.

(d) In any proceeding brought by the Commission under subsection (b), except as provided in subsection (c) of this section, the defendant may petition the court for an order modifying or setting aside the demand of the Commission.

SEC. 711. (a) Every employer, employment agency, and labor organization, as the case may be, shall post and keep posted in conspicuous places upon its premises where notices to employees, applicants for employment, and members are customarily posted a notice to be prepared or approved by the Commission setting forth excerpts from or, summaries of, the pertinent provisions of this title and information pertinent to the filing of a complaint.

(b) A willful violation of this section shall be punishable by a fine of not more than $100 for each separate offense.

VETERANS' PREFERENCE

SEC. 712. Nothing contained in this title shall be construed to repeal or modify any Federal, State, territorial, or local law creating special rights or preference for veterans.

RULES AND REGULATIONS

SEC. 713. (a) The Commission shall have authority from time to time to issue, amend, or rescind suitable procedural regulations to carry out the provisions of this title. Regulations issued under this section shall be in conformity with the standards and limitations of the Administrative Procedure Act.

(b) In any action or proceeding based on any alleged unlawful employment practice, no person shall be subject to any liability or punishment for or on account of (1) the commission by such person of an unlawful employment practice if he pleads and proves that the act or omission complained of was in good faith, in conformity with, and in reliance on any written interpretation or opinion of the Commission, or (2) the failure of such person to publish and file any information required by any provision of this title if he pleads and proves that he failed to publish and file such information in good faith, in conformity with the instructions of the Commission issued under this title regarding the filing of such information. Such a defense, if established, shall be a bar to the action or proceeding, notwithstanding that (A) after such act or omission, such interpretation or opinion is modified or rescinded or is determined by judicial authority to be invalid or of no legal effect, or (B) after publishing or filing the description and annual reports, such publication or filing is determined by judicial authority not to be in conformity with the requirements of this title.

FORCIBLY RESISTING THE COMMISSION OR ITS REPRESENTATIVES

SEC. 714. The provisions of section 111, title 18, United States Code, shall apply to officers, agents, and employees of the Commission in the performance of their official duties.

SPECIAL STUDY BY SECRETARY OF LABOR

SEC. 715. The Secretary of Labor shall make a full and complete study of the factors which might tend to result in discrimination in employment because of age and of the consequences of such discrimination on the economy and individuals affected. The Secretary of Labor shall make a report to the Congress not later than June 30, 1965, containing the results of such study and shall include in such report such recommendations for legislation to prevent arbitrary discrimination in employment because of age as he determines advisable.

EFFECTIVE DATE

SEC. 716. (a) This title shall become effective one year after the date of its enactment.
(b) Notwithstanding subsection (a), sections of this title other than sections 703, 704, 706, and 707 shall become effective immediately.
(c) The President shall, as soon as feasible after the enactment of this title, convene one or more conferences for the purpose of enabling the leaders of groups whose members will be affected by this title to become familiar with the rights afforded and obligations imposed by its provisions, and for the purpose of making plans which will result in the fair and effective administration of this title when all of its provisions become effective. The President shall invite the participation in such conference or conferences of (1) the members of the President's Committee on Equal Employment Opportunity, (2) the members of the Commission on Civil Rights, (3) representatives of State and local agencies engaged in furthering equal employment opportunity, (4) representatives of private agencies engaged in furthering equal employment opportunity, and (5) representatives of employers, labor organizations, and employment agencies who will be subject to this title.

TITLE VIII—REGISTRATION AND VOTING STATISTICS

SEC. 801. The Secretary of Commerce shall promptly conduct a survey to compile registration and voting statistics in such geographic areas as may be recommended by the Commission on Civil Rights. Such a survey and compilation shall, to the extent recommended by the Commission on Civil Rights, only include a count of persons of voting age by race, color, and national origin, and determination of the extent to which such persons are registered to vote, and have voted in any statewide primary or general election in which the Members of the United States House of Representatives are nominated or elected, since January 1, 1960. Such information shall also be collected and compiled in connection with the Nineteenth Decennial Census, and at such other times as the Congress may prescribe. The provisions of section 9 and chapter 7 of title 13, United States Code, shall apply to any survey, collection, or compilation of registration and voting statistics carried out under this title: Provided, however, That no person shall be compelled to disclose his race, color, national origin, or questioned about his political party affiliation, how he voted, or the reasons therefore, nor shall any penalty be imposed for his failure or refusal to make such disclosure. Every person interrogated orally, by written survey or questionnaire or by any other means with respect to such information shall be fully advised with respect to his right to fail or refuse to furnish such information.

TITLE IX—INTERVENTION AND PROCEDURE AFTER REMOVAL IN CIVIL RIGHTS CASES

SEC. 901. Title 28 of the United States Code, section 1447(d), is amended to read as follows:

"An order remanding a case to the State court from which it was removed is not reviewable on appeal or otherwise, except that an order remanding a case to the State court from which it was removed pursuant to section 1443 of this title shall be reviewable by appeal or otherwise."

SEC. 902. Whenever an action has been commenced in any court of the United States seeking relief from the denial of equal protection of the laws under the fourteenth amendment to the Constitution on account of race, color, religion, or national origin, the Attorney General for or in the name of the United States may intervene in such action upon timely application if the Attorney General certifies that the case is of general public importance. In such action the United States shall be entitled to the same relief as if it had instituted the action.

TITLE X—ESTABLISHMENT OF COMMUNITY RELATIONS SERVICE

SEC. 1001. (a) There is hereby established in and as a part of the Department of Commerce a Community Relations Service (hereinafter referred to as the "Service"), which shall be headed by a Director who shall be appointed by the President with the advice and consent of the Senate for a term of four years. The Director is authorized to appoint, subject to the civil service laws and regulations, such other personnel as may be necessary to enable the Service to carry out its functions and duties, and to fix their compensation in accordance with the Classification Act of 1949, as amended. The Director is further authorized to procure services as authorized by section 15 of the Act of August 2, 1946 (60 Stat. 810; 5 U.S.C. 55(a)), but at rates for individuals not in excess of $75 per diem.

(b) Section 106(a) of the Federal Executive Pay Act of 1956, as amended (5 U.S.C. 2205(a)), is further amended by adding the following clause thereto:

"(52) Director, Community Relations Service."

SEC. 1002. It shall be the function of the Service to provide assistance to communities and persons therein in resolving disputes, disagreements, or difficulties relating to discriminatory practices based on race, color, or national origin which impair the rights of persons in such communities under the Constitution or laws of the United States or which affect or may affect interstate commerce. The Service may offer its services in cases of such disputes, disagreements, or difficulties whenever, in its judgment, peaceful relations among the citizens of the community involved are threatened thereby, and it may offer its services either upon its own motion or upon the request of an appropriate State or local official or other interested person.

SEC. 1003. (a) The Service shall, whenever possible, in performing its functions, seek and utilize the cooperation of appropriate State or local, public, or private agencies.

(b) The activities of all officers and employees of the Service in providing conciliation assistance shall be conducted in confidence and without publicity, and the Service shall hold confidential any information acquired in the regular performance of its duties upon the understanding that it would be so held. No officer or employee of the Service shall engage in the performance of investigative or prosecuting functions of any department or agency in any litigation arising out of a dispute in which he acted on behalf of the Service. Any officer or other employee of the Service, who shall make public in any manner whatever any information in violation of this subsection, shall be deemed guilty of a misdemeanor and, upon conviction thereof, shall be fined not more than $1,000 or imprisoned not more than one year.

SEC. 1004. Subject to the provisions of sections 205 and 1003(b), the Director shall, on or before January 31 of each year, submit to the Congress a report of the activities of the Service during the preceding fiscal year.

TITLE XI—MISCELLANEOUS

SEC. 1101. In any proceeding for criminal contempt arising under title II, III, IV, V, VI, or VII of this Act, the accused, upon demand therefor, shall be entitled to a trial by jury, which shall conform as near as may be to the practice in criminal cases. Upon conviction, the accused shall not be fined more than $1,000 or imprisoned for more than six months. This section shall not apply to contempts committed in the presence of the court, or so near thereto as to obstruct the administration of justice, nor to the misbehavior, misconduct, or disobedience of any officer of the court in respect to writs, orders, or process of the court. No person shall be convicted of criminal contempt hereunder unless the act or omission constituting such contempt shall have been intentional, as required in other cases of criminal contempt.

Nor shall anything herein be construed to deprive courts of their power, by civil contempt proceedings, without a jury, to secure compliance with or to prevent obstruction of, as distinguished from punishment for violations of, any lawful writ, process, order, rule, decree, or command of the court in accordance with the prevailing usages of law and equity, including the power of detention.

SEC. 1102. No person should be put twice in jeopardy under the laws of the United States for the same act or omission. For this reason, an acquittal or conviction in a prosecution for a specific crime under the laws of the United States shall bar a proceeding for criminal contempt, which is based upon the same act or omission and which arises under the provisions of this Act; and an acquittal or conviction in a proceeding for criminal contempt, which arises under the provisions of this Act, shall bar a prosecution for a specific crime under the laws of the United States based upon the same act or omission.

SEC. 1103. Nothing in this Act shall be construed to deny, impair, or otherwise affect any right or authority of the Attorney General or of the United States or any agency or officer thereof under existing law to institute or intervene in any action or proceeding.

SEC. 1104. Nothing contained in any title of this Act shall be construed as indicating an intent on the part of Congress to occupy the field in which any such title operates to the exclusion of State laws on the same

subject matter, nor shall any provision of this Act be construed as invalidating any provision of State law unless such provision is inconsistent with any of the purposes of this Act, or any provision thereof.
SEC. 1105. There are hereby authorized to be appropriated such sums as are necessary to carry out the provisions of this Act.
SEC. 1106. If any provision of this Act or the application thereof to any person or circumstances is held invalid, the remainder of the Act and the application of the provision to other persons not similarly situated or to other circumstances shall not be affected thereby.
Approved July 2, 1964.
Transcription courtesy of the Avalon Project at Yale Law School.

Tennessee's State Laws

Americans with Disabilities Act—ADA
Child Labor Act
Discrimination
Employment-At-Will
Family and Medical Leave Act—FMLA
Last Wages Due Deceased Employee

AMERICANS WITH DISABILITIES ACT—ADA

What if I have a complaint about unfair labor practices?
Applicants for employment or employees having disabilities may be protected against employment discrimination by the Americans with Disabilities Act, or ADA. Those needing information about ADA may visit the Job Accommodation Network
(JAN) Website.

To Top

CHILD LABOR ACT Title 50-5-101-115

My child is 15 and wants to work. Where do I get a work permit?
The state of Tennessee does not require work permits. The minor needs to provide the prospective employer with a copy one of the following documents as proof of age; birth certificate, driver license, state issued ID, or a copy of their passport.

What is the age a child can go to work? Are there any restrictions?
In Tennessee, a minor must be 14 years of age before they can work. Some of the restrictions for 14 and 15-year-old minors are:

WHEN SCHOOL IS IN SESSION:
Can work no more than 3 hours per day
Can work no more than 18 hours a week
Can work no later than 7:00 pm.

WHEN SCHOOL IS NOT IN SESSION:
Can work no more than 8 hours a day
Can work no more than 40 hours per week
Can work no later than 9:00 pm.

Breaks for minors under age 18:
Any minor scheduled to work 6 hours must have a thirty (30) minute rest or meal break no exceptions.

Are these restrictions the same for 16 and 17 year old?
No. There are no limitations on the number of hours that 16 and 17-year-old minors work. They cannot be required to work during school hours; nor can they work past 10:00 pm. on nights preceding school days (Sunday through Thursday nights), unless their parents or guardians sign a Parental Consent Form. The Parental Consent Form would allow them to work no later than 12:00 midnight three of those nights while school is in session.

The Child Labor Act prohibits minors, whether they are 14 to 15 or 16 to 17 year old from employment in certain occupations. A copy of the Child Labor Act may be obtained upon request. Note: State and Federal Laws conflict. Therefore, we have quoted the stricter of the two laws.

To Top

DISCRIMINATION

How do I file a claim for discriminatory practices?

Discrimination against employees is illegal under both Federal and State law. Employers may not discriminate against an employee on the basis of the employee's race, sex, age, religion, color, national origin or disability.
Claims of discrimination in Tennessee should be forwarded either to the Tennessee Commission on Human Rights in Nashville Tennessee at (615) 741-5825,
or to the Equal Employment Opportunity Commission (EEOC) in Nashville, Tennessee. You may visit the TCHR Web site and the EEOC Web site.
Pregnancy Discrimination
Tennessee also has a specific pregnancy discrimination law (Tennessee Revised Statute Title 4-21-408) that prohibits an employer from discriminating against a pregnant employee. These complaints should be forwarded to TCHR or EEOC.

To Top

EMPLOYMENT-AT-WILL

Are there any legal restrictions against firing, suspending or disciplining employees?

Tennessee is known as an "EMPLOYMENT-AT-WILL" state. Generally, this means that an employer may legally hire, fire, suspend or discipline any employee at any time and for any reason—good or bad—or for no reason at all. However, an employer may not discriminate against any employee on the basis of the employee's race, sex, age, religion, color, national origin, or disability.

Also, under the Tennessee "WHISTLE BLOWER'S LAW", the employer may not take any
reprisal against an employee who advises the employer that the business is in violation of a law and the employee either discloses, threatens to disclose, or testifies about the violation of law, or the employee objects to or refuses to participate in an employment act in violation of law. This law may be found at Tennessee Revised Statutes Title 50-1-304.

There are other exceptions to Tennessee's "EMPLOYMENT-AT-WILL" doctrine. Tennessee employees may not be disciplined or discharged at-will for:

Being called to military service Title 8-33-101 thru 8-33-109

Voting in elections Title 2-1-106
Exercising right of association Title 50-1-201 thru 50-1-204
Wage garnishment Title 26-2-101 thru 26-2-410
Filing workers' compensation claim Title 50-6-101 thru 50-6-705
Being called to jury duty Title 22-4-108
(Employer must also pay the employee wages during the jury service less what the court pays.)

Employees who are fired may still apply for unemployment insurance benefits. The Tennessee Department of Labor and Workforce Development's Unemployment Insurance
Division will determine eligibility. Further information may be found under the Unemployment Insurance section of this web site.

To Top

FAMILY AND MEDICAL LEAVE ACT—FMLA

Under the Family and Medical Leave Act, or FMLA, employers having 50 or more employees must grant medical leave to some employees in certain circumstances without the threat of the loss of their job. Questions concerning the
enforcement of FMLA matters should be directed to the FMLA section of the United States Department of Labor's Web site.

Can an employee be discharged while out sick even though they provide a doctor's statement?

There are no Tennessee laws regulating terminations. If the employee feels discrimination is involved, they are referred to either the Tennessee Human Rights Commission or the Equal Employment Opportunity Commission.

To Top

LAST WAGES DUE DECEASED EMPLOYEE

Under certain circumstances, Tennessee law allows employers to pay to the surviving spouse or children of a deceased employee the last wages and other benefits due the deceased employee without a court order. This law may be found at Tennessee Revised Statutes Title 30-2-103

To Top

NATIONAL LABOR RELATIONS BOARD—NLRB

Questions concerning unfair labor practices where a union is involved should be directed to the National Labor Relations Board (NLRB) at their Web site.

To Top

Questions Concerning a PENSION or 401(k) plan

Questions concerning an employee's failure to be able to collect their pension or money from a 401(k) plan should be directed to the EBSA (formerly PWBA) section of the United States Department of Labor's web site.

To Top

PREVAILING WAGE ACT Title 12-4-401 (Part 4)

I am working on a state-funded Prevailing Wage Project? I am performing the duties of a carpenter but not being paid the correct wages. Can you help me?
Yes. All contractors on state-funded projects are required to post the wage rate on the job-site and pay the correct rate of pay for each craft they perform.

Does the Department of Labor and Workforce Development make on-site inspections?
Yes. On-site inspections are made and employees are interviewed to see if they are being paid the correct rate for the job they are performing. We check to be sure that the wage rate is posted for all employees to verify they are paid the correct wage rates.

Who sets the prevailing wage rates?
The Prevailing Wage Commission sets the rates on highway projects every year and
on building projects every other year. Both are based on a survey of each industry. For Current Highway Rates or Current Building Rates and Regions see web site.

If a contractor has not paid the prevailing wage rate, what can be done?
All claims are investigated and if violations are found, the contractor is required to pay the prevailing wage plus any back wages due.

To Top

REQUIRED POSTERS

Does Tennessee require labor laws to be posted?
Yes. See "Required Posters" to view or for copies.

To Top

UNAUTHORIZED DEDUCTIONS FROM PAYCHECK

Under Tennessee law deductions can only be taken out of pay if the employee has authorized it by a written statement.

To Top

Questions Concerning Overtime, Minimum Wage, or Salaried Employees

Tennessee has no wage laws concerning overtime, minimum wage, or the regulation
of salaried employees. The United States Department of Labor's Wage and Hour Division enforces the Fair Labor Standards Act regulating minimum wage, overtime and salaried employees. Further information concerning these matters may be found at the WH division of the Department of Labor web site.

To Top

TENNESSEE WAGE REGULATION ACT Title 50-2-101

What is the law concerning payment of final paychecks to employees?
Tennessee employees who are laid off, fired, or who quit must be paid their wages in full at the next regular payday, not to exceed 21 days from the date of their discharge or termination. Claims against an employer for late payment may be filed with the Labor Standards Division. The Tennessee Department of Labor and Workforce Development has the authority to enforce this law. You may review this law at Tennessee Revised Statutes Title 50-2-103(g)

Isn't my employer required to provide breaks and a meal period?
State law requires that each employee scheduled to work six (6) consecutive hours must have a thirty (30) minute meal or rest period, except in workplace environments that by their nature of business provides for ample opportunity to rest or take an appropriate break. The failure to give a (30) minute meal or rest period is a violation of State law only. There are no State or Federal requirements for additional breaks. The Federal Law does require breaks of less than 30 minutes in duration to be paid if the employer chooses to grant such breaks. Title 50-2-103 (h)

How often must my employer pay me?
All wages or compensation of employees in private employment is due and payable at least semi-monthly and notice of regular paydays must be posted by each employer in at least two conspicuous places. Title 50-2-103

Retail Shrink 101

My employer has just told me he is going to cut my pay. Can he do this without my approval?
An employee's pay can be cut with or without his approval as long as the employer tells the employee BEFORE any work is done. The employee cannot work without first knowing the amount of wages to be paid. Title 50-2-101

Under Tennessee Wage Regulation Act Title 50-2-101-50-2-108, an employer is prohibited from penalizing an employee or deducting any sum of money as a penalty or fine from the employee's wages.

Tennessee Wage Regulation Act Title 50-2-103 requires employers of private employments of 5 or more employees to establish and maintain regular pay periods at least twice monthly. Penalties may be accessed for violation of this section against those employers for missing a regularly scheduled payroll date and in paying their employees late.

Can my employer hold my paycheck until I return my uniform, etc.?
No. An employer cannot hold your paycheck for any reason.
Can my employer withhold the cost of my uniform, equipment, company loans, shortages and negligence, etc. from my paycheck?
No. Your employer cannot make any deductions from your paycheck without your consent to the deductions.

I work in the same job classification as a person of the opposite sex, but I am paid less. Is this legal?
No employer shall discriminate between employees in the same establishment on the basis of sex by paying one employee more or less than he pays to any employee of the opposite sex for comparable skill, effort and responsibility in which they are performed under similar working conditions. However, nothing prohibits wage deferential based on a seniority system, a merit system, a system which measures earnings by quality production or any other reasonable deferential which is based on a factor other than sex. Title 50-2-201 thru 207

If I complain about equal pay, whose wages would be adjusted?
An employer who is paying a wage deferential in violation of the act shall not reduce the wages of any employee in order to be in compliance.

Can an employer terminate an employee for a claim on equal pay?
No employer is allowed to terminate or discriminate against any employee who files a claim for equal pay.

Is an employer required by law to provide paid vacation, holidays, severance pay, sick pay or health insurance?
No. The State of Tennessee does not have a law that regulates fringe benefits. Company policy would be the determining factor. These and similar matters are also determined by an agreement between the employees and the employer, or their
authorized representatives. Title 50-2-103 (3)

If an employer's policy provides a paid vacation and the employee's employment is terminated, is the employer required to compensate for any vacation time I have accrued but not used?

No. Unless the employer's policy or its labor agreement specifically requires compensation of unused "vacation pay or other compensatory time" to an employee upon his or her termination of employment, Tennessee Code Annotated § 50-2-103(a)(3) does not require that an employee's final wages include such compensation.

If an employee terminates voluntarily or involuntarily, does the employer have to pay all wages due at the time of termination?
The employer is required to pay all wages or compensation due the terminated employee on the next regular payday following the date of termination or 21 days thereafter, whichever comes last.

If the employer refuses payment of wages, what can the employee do?
Anyone who has a problem collecting wages can file a wage claim with the Tennessee Department of Labor and Workforce Development's Division of Labor Standards. If the circumstances are such that we are unable to help, the complainant is referred to court.

If an employee is still employed and the employer is not paying the employee correctly and they file a wage claim, can they be terminated?
There is no Tennessee law which prevents an employer from firing an employee because they file a complaint with our office, unless the complaint was equal pay.

Who determines how many hours a part-time employee may work and how long may an employee be consider part-time?
The employer sets the number of hours and makes the decision when the employee becomes a permanent employee.

My employer has just told me that I am going to be paid by direct deposit. Can he do this?
Yes, an employer can change the method of payment to direct deposit. However, the choice of the financial institution must be that of the employee.

To Top

WHO ENFORCES STATE LABOR LAWS?

The Tennessee Department of Labor and Workforce Development, Labor Standards Division, has jurisdiction to enforce the Following State Labor Laws:
Child Labor Laws Title 50-5-101 thru 115
Prevailing Wage Act Title 12-4-401 thru 415

Wage Regulation Act Title 50-2-101 thru 109

Only questions that arise in each of the above areas should be directed to the Labor Standards Division. All other questions should be directed to the proper agency (see previous sections) or to an attorney or a labor, employment, or human resources consultant.

Does TDLWD provide advice on garnishments, tax levies, or other similar withholding's from pay?TDLWD does not have the authority to provide assistance or advice in this area.

Will TDLWD provide me with legal representation or advice?
The TDLWD Legal Division provides legal services to TDLWD and its offices and employees only. The Legal Division does not offer legal representation, legal opinions or legal advice to the general public. It is recommended those individuals seeking personal counsel request the assistance of a private attorney or Legal Services Corporation.

As an employer must I provide a former or current employee with a copy of my employment personnel files?
There's no federal law or Tennessee law that requires the employer to do so. The employment file is the property of the employer. The employer is not required to furnish current or former employee's whole file or specific things in the file.

However, the employer may choose to furnish a copy. If the employee files suit, they will be able to subpoena the file any way. An employer may charge for example, 50 cents a page, to cover time and cost to copy, payable up front in cash. Example, the person requesting the file should be told how many pages are in the file. If the file consists of fifty pages, they would have to present the employer with $25.00 before the file would be copied

WORK CITED

"What's True About False Arrests?", By Patricia A. Patrick and Shaun L. Gabbidon

ASIS International, Inc. Worldwide Headquarters, 1625 Prince Street, Alexandria, Virginia 22314-2818 U.S.A. 703.519.6200 | fax 703.519.6299 | http://www.asisonline.org/

http://www.ourdocuments.gov/doc-U.S. National Archives & Records Administration
700 Pennsylvania Avenue NW, Washington, DC 20408 •
1-86-NARA-NARA •
1-866-272-6272

http://www.TN.gov-Department of Labor and Workforce Development
220 French Landing Drive
Nashville, Tennessee 37243
(615) 741-6642

US Constitution Bill of Rights—U_S_ Government Info-Resources.htm

Transcript of Civil Rights Act (1964) (print-friendly version) www.ourdocuments.govApril 18, 2013

Author Joel Santana born in a small town in the state of Michigan has had a successful career in the field of retail management. His proven shrink record speaks volumes over his career. A Graduate of SAE Institute of Technology graduating at the top of his class in Audio Technology, and his Degree in Business Technology gives readers over 10 years or retail management experience. In this book he shows how important shrink is to him and his willingness to give back all that he has learned over the years. He realizes managing a retail store is merely half the battle, reaching beyond company goals and personal goals is the real test of life and time.

www.ingramcontent.com/pod-product-compliance
Lightning Source LLC
Chambersburg PA
CBHW030905180526
45163CB00004B/1709